Contemporary Irish Monologues

THE EDITC

Jim Culleto ... Director of Fishamble Theatre Company and has worked in theatres including the Abbey, the Gate and the Coliseum. He has also directed for Pigsback, the Passion Machine, 7:84 (Scotland), Project Arts Centre, Amharclann de hÍde, the Ark and Second Age.

Clodagh O'Donoghue is an actor who has worked with the Abbey, Fishamble, Project Arts Centre, Second Age, Pigsback, RTE and BBC. She also works as an abstract writer and has written and told her own stories for children on RTE television.

They have taught in universities and drama schools throughout Ireland and Europe.

Acknowledgements

All the playwrights, agents and publishers for permission to use play excerpts, Ciara Considine, Edwin Higel and all at New Island Books, Dermot Bolger, Joe Dowling, Liam and Dolores Culleton, Seán and Doreen O'Donoghue, Fishamble Theatre Company, Maureen Kennelly, Gavin Kostick, Siobhán Maguire, Marty Bennett, Lynne Parker, Pat Kinevane, Marion O'Dwyer, Patrick Sutton, Peter McAllister, Betty-Ann Norton, Caroline FitzGerald, Noelle Brown, Anna Culleton, Garry White, Karen Ardiff, Deirdre Molloy, Alan Gray, Sarah Clarke, Brian Fay, Kathy Koenigsmark, Orla Martin, Jo Mangan, Nick Marston, Leah Schmidt, Wendy Gresser, Julia Tyrrell, Pauline Asper, Maureen McGlynn.

CONTEMPORARY IRISH MONOLOGUES

60 AUDITION SPEECHES FOR MEN AND WOMEN

Edited by JIM CULLETON
and CLODAGH O'DONOGHUE

Introduced by JOE DOWLING

First published in Ireland by New Island Books, 2 Brookside, Dundrum Road, Dublin 14, Ireland.

A CIP catalogue record for this book is available from the British Library.
ISBN: 1 874597 92 8
Printed and bound in Great Britain by Cox & Wyman Ltd., Reading, Berkshire.

New Island Books receives financial assistance from The Arts Council (An Chomairle Ealaíon), Dublin, Ireland.

ACKNOWLEDGEMENTS
Grateful acknowledgement is made for permission to reprint extracts from copyrighted material:

A Crucial Week in the Life of a Grocer's Assistant by Tom Murphy, copyright © 1978, 1989 Tom Murphy, Methuen Publishing Ltd, 215 Vauxhall Bridge Road, London SW1V 1EJ, England. **A Handful of Stars** by Billy Roche copyright © 1989, 1992 Billy Roche, Nick Hern Books, 14 Larden Road, London W3 7ST, England. **A Night in November** by Marie Jones copyright © 1995 Marie Jones, New Island Books, 2 Brookside, Dundrum Road, Dublin 14, Ireland. **A Picture of Paradise** by Jimmy Murphy copyright © 1996 Jimmy Murphy, 6 Woodfield Place, Inchicore, Dublin 8, Ireland. **Aristocrats** by Brian Friel copyright © 1980 Brian Friel, Faber and Faber, 3 Queen Square, London WC1N 3AU, England. **At the Black Pig's Dyke** by Vincent Woods, copyright © 1998 Vincent Woods, Methuen Publishing Ltd, 215 Vauxhall Bridge Road, London SW1V 1EJ, England. **Bailegangaire** by Tom Murphy, copyright © 1986, 1988, 1993 Tom Murphy, Methuen Publishing Ltd, 215 Vauxhall Bridge Road, London SW1V 1EJ, England. **Bat the Father, Rabbit the Son** by Donal O'Kelly copyright © 1998 Donal O'Kelly, Methuen Publishing Ltd, 215 Vauxhall Bridge Road, London SW1V 1EJ, England. **Belfry** by Billy Roche copyright © 1992 Billy Roche, Nick Hern Books, 14 Larden Road, London W3 7ST, England. **Big Maggie** by John B Keane, copyright © 1990 John B Keane, Mercier Press Limited, PO Box 5, 5 French Church Street, Cork, Ireland. **Carthaginians** by Frank McGuinness copyright © 1988, 1996 Frank McGuinness, Faber and Faber, 3 Queen Square, London

Contents

Editors' Introduction xi

Preface by Joe Dowling xii

Monologues for Women

1 The Sanctuary Lamp **by Tom Murphy** 2
2 Lovers: Winners **by Brian Friel** 4
3 Disco Pigs **by Enda Walsh** 6
4 Joyriders **by Christina Reid** 8
5 Sucking Dublin **by Enda Walsh** 10
6 Our Lady of Sligo **by Sebastian Barry** 12
7 Translations **by Brian Friel** 14
8 The Dogs **by Donal O'Kelly** 16
9 Digging for Fire **by Declan Hughes** 18
10 The Mai **by Marina Carr** 20
11 Portia Coughlan **by Marina Carr** 22
12 New Morning **by Declan Hughes** 24
13 Pentecost **by Stewart Parker** 26
14 The Weir **by Conor McPherson** 28
15 One Last White Horse **by Dermot Bolger** 32
16 Twinkletoes **by Jennifer Johnston** 34
17 The Only True History of Lizzie Finn **by Sebastian Barry** 38
18 Belfry **by Billy Roche** 40
19 Dancing at Lughnasa **by Brian Friel** 42
20 Bailegangaire **by Tom Murphy** 44
21 The Beauty Queen of Leenane **by Martin McDonagh** 46
22 Molly Sweeney **by Brian Friel** 48
23 Stella by Starlight **by Bernard Farrell** 52
24 Mrs Sweeney **by Paula Meehan** 54
25 At the Black Pig's Dyke **by Vincent Woods** 56
26 Carthaginians **by Frank McGuinness** 58
27 Too Late For Logic **by Tom Murphy** 60
28 Donny Boy **by Robin Glendinning** 62
29 Big Maggie **by John B. Keane** 64
30 The Desert Lullaby **by Jennifer Johnston** 66

Monologues for Men

1 Belfry **by Billy Roche** 70

2 The Cripple of Inishmaan **by Martin McDonagh** 72

3 This Lime Tree Bower **by Conor McPherson** 74

4 A Handful of Stars **by Billy Roche** 76

5 Howie the Rookie **by Mark O'Rowe** 78

6 Red Roses and Petrol **by Joseph O'Connor** 80

7 Home **by Paul Mercier** 82

8 Good Evening, Mr Collins **by Tom McIntyre** 84

9 Hubert Murray's Widow **by Michael Harding** 86

10 In High Germany **by Dermot Bolger** 88

11 Long Black Coat **by John Waters** 90

12 Donny Boy **by Robin Glendinning** 92

13 Observe the Sons of Ulster Marching Towards the Somme **by Frank McGuinness** 94

14 A Crucial Week in the Life of a Grocer's Assistant **by Tom Murphy** 96

15 Pentecost **by Stewart Parker** 98

16 A Night in November **by Marie Jones** 100

17 Bat the Father, Rabbit the Son **by Donal O'Kelly** 102

18 Hard to Believe **by Conall Morrison** 104

19 Aristocrats **by Brian Friel** 106

20 Prayers of Sherkin **by Sebastian Barry** 108

21 Faith Healer **by Brian Friel** 110

22 Moonshine **by Jim Nolan** 112

23 A Picture of Paradise **by Jimmy Murphy** 114

24 The Field **by John B. Keane** 116

25 Lovers: Losers **by Brian Friel** 118

26 The Gigli Concert **by Tom Murphy** 120

27 Down Onto Blue **by Pom Boyd** 122

28 King of the Castle **by Eugene McCabe** 124

29 Talbot's Box **by Thomas Kilroy** 126

30 The Steward of Christendom **by Sebastian Barry** 128

For Daniel

Editors' Introduction

There are many audition/monologue books available, especially some excellent collections of speeches from classical, British and American drama. There is no book of Irish monologues, however, to help students and actors looking for an Irish speech to perform for an audition or exam. This book came about because of a perceived need for such a collection of pieces. It is intended as a resource for acting students, teachers, actors and directors.

The 1960s saw the emergence of major playwrights still at the centre of Irish theatre today – as well as changing attitudes in Ireland towards many aspects of public and private life. Monologues for this contemporary collection were chosen therefore from plays written between mid-1960s and late-1990s, although the emphasis is placed on plays written during the last decade. This is so that the book can give both as comprehensive and up-to-date an impression of contemporary Irish drama as possible, and is as representative of the vibrant theatre scene as it can be – although obviously some prolific playwrights have not written monologues that suit an anthology such as this.

The criteria we applied for inclusion were that each speech should last approximately 2 to 3 minutes in duration and be self-contained enough to work out-of-context for audition purposes. 60 monologues (30 for men and 30 for women) are arranged according to the age of the characters – where an age is not stated, the monologue is placed in an appropriate position among the other speeches. The symbol (...) represents a break in the original text where another character speaks. It was necessary that each play included had been published at the time of permissions being sought for this selection so that the entire play is available to be read.

We hope you enjoy reading the monologues and the plays from which they come.

Jim Culleton and Clodagh O'Donoghue
October 1999

Preface

There must be a fairer, more democratic and satisfying way of casting a play than the imperfect system of auditions. Talented people are obliged to show their worth for ten minutes and from that brief encounter, directors and producers are expected to judge their suitability for a major role. Some really talented actors do not audition well while others shine for a brief time but cannot sustain the performance over a longer period. It is the same the world over. However much we may wish for an alternative system, no one has yet come up with the ideal casting method that does not involve hearing the actor read or perform a monologue or read a scene from the play being cast.

Given how unfair the system is and how stressful it can be for actors, it is a joy to find a book designed to help make life easier for the Irish actor. One of the things that makes this book so exciting is that each of the monologues is perfectly chosen to suit the audition process. A valuable piece of advice for young actors is to choose a piece that has a self-contained context. A speech that refers to things revealed in the previous scenes but not explained can be confusing for the poor director who has listened to dozens of speeches that day. Choosing a speech with a huge emotional climax may seem like a good idea to show your range but, unless the director has a detailed knowledge of the play, it may just seem like an empty and over-the-top rant. The overheated Ophelia or the out of control Romeo is not always the best choice to make a first impression.

Irish theatre has changed so dramatically in the last thirty years. It is fascinating to see those changes reflected in the choices made by the editors. From the hilarity and pathos of Tom Murphy's 1968 Abbey hit, *A Crucial Week in the Life of a Grocer's Assistant* to the chilling and exquisite writing of Conor McPherson's *The Weir*, Irish writers continue to create a vibrant and diverse way of telling their stories. The strength of this valuable collection is that each of the selections is from a storyteller with great creativity. There is also a real sense of the power and complexity of Irish writing during the last thirty years. It is the quality of our writers that keeps Irish theatre at the centre of world drama. This book is a welcome reminder of a golden time in Irish theatre as well as a practical handbook for the unfortunate actors who must endure the hated audition process.

Joe Dowling
Artistic Director
The Guthrie Theater
Minneapolis, MN

30 MONOLOGUES FOR WOMEN

Maudie is a waif-like girl in her mid-teens who has been brought up by a reluctant grandmother and a hostile grandfather. She has taken shelter for the night in a city church. She is joined by Francisco – another lost soul. Here, she decides to confide in him.

The Sanctuary Lamp *by Tom Murphy*

Maudie

Do you know – hospitals? Well, my grandad said let someone else take care of me. Well, I come home late one night and he were waiting. In the hall. In his bare feet. And he found eight new p. in my pocket. *I* don't know how it got there. Maybe one of the bigger boys. And grandad said he would have kicked me, if he had his boots on. And grandad said let someone else take care of me to have a baby. And gran was lucky to find me one of those hospitals. And I had a baby. I knew he were not well. But I knew if I could not take care of him, who could? And once I woke and they were taking him away. And I growled. But there were an old – Do you know nuns? Well, there were an old nun. She were in black, the others were in white, and she were my friend. And she said had I thought of a name for him. *I* hadn't thought of a name. And she said would I call him Stephen. Because that were her name. And she would like that. And I said okay. And they smiled – the way I said 'okay'. And I laughed. But I were not happy at all. But I were so warm and sleepy. I wanted to sit up so they'd see I were not happy. Because I were crying. So they took him away to baptize him. Because he were not well. And the next time I woke up, only the old nun were there. And she come to me, sort of smiling and frowning together. And she said 'Maudie. Maudie.' Like that. Like as if I were asleep. But I were awake. I were wide awake. And she said, 'Stephen is dead, Maudie. Stephen is with Jesus'. At first I didn't know if she were only fibbing, but when he started to visit me – No, not dreaming! Not dreaming! So all around me! – I knew he were dead alright. But I didn't tell them. Because I wanted them to let me go. And I didn't want the other patients to pull my hair. I only told the old nun. To ask her would it stop. And she said it would, in time. And I said, when I got forgiveness, was it? And she said yes.

Mag is a vivacious seventeen-year-old, filled with enthusiasm for life. She is pregnant and due to be married to Joe in three weeks. They have both come to a hill overlooking Ballymore to study for their final school examinations. Joe is the more serious of the two and is making a valiant effort to study. Mag continues chatting to him, even though she knows he is not listening.

Lovers: Winners *by Brian Friel*

Mag

I can see the boarders out on the tennis courts. They should be studying. And there's a funeral going up High Street; nine cars, and a petrol lorry, and an ambulance. Maybe the deceased was run over by the petrol lorry – the father of a large family – and the driver is paying his respects and crying his eyes out. If he doesn't stop blubbering, he'll run over someone else. And the widow is in the ambulance, all in plaster, crippled for life. (*She tries out a mime of this – both arms and legs cast in awkward shapes*) And the children are going to be farmed out to cruel aunts with squints and moustaches. Sister Michael has a beard. Joan O'Hara says she shaves with a cut-throat every first Friday and uses an after-shave lotion called Virility. God, nuns are screams if you don't take them seriously. I think I'd rather be a widow than a widower; but I'd rather be a bachelor than a spinster. And I'd rather be deaf than dumb; but I'd rather be dumb than blind. And if I had to choose between lung cancer, a coronary, and multiple sclerosis, I'd take the coronary. Papa's family all died of coronaries, long before they were commonplace. (*She sits up to tell the following piece of family history*) He had a sister, Nan, who used to sing at the parochial concert every Christmas; and one year, when she was singing *Jerusalem* – you know, just before the chorus, when the piano is panting Huh-huh-huh-huh-huh-huh, she opened her mouth and dropped like a log …

Joe, d'you think (*quoting something she has read*) my legs have got thick, my body gross, my facial expression passive to dull, and my eyes lack-lustre? I hope it's a boy, and that it'll be like you – with a great big bursting brain. Or maybe it'll be twins – like me. I wonder what Peter would have been like? Sometimes when she's very ill Mother calls me Peter. If it were going to be twins I'd rather have a boy and a girl than two boys or two girls; but if it were going to be triplets I'd rather have two boys and a girl or two girls and a boy than three boys or three girls. (*Very wisely and directed to Joe*) And I have a feeling it's going to be premature.

Runt and Pig – named Sinéad and Darren by their parents – were born on the same day. They have reached the age of seventeen as inseparable friends. They have created a violent world for themselves and communicate in their own special language. Runt now feels, however, that the nature of their relationship is changing. In a fast food restaurant in Cork City, she shares her thoughts with the audience.

Disco Pigs *by Enda Walsh*

Runt

Our two mams all sweety an stinkin a new born babas n' blood! I member open an look my eyes an ja see a liddle baba in the nex bed. An dat liddle baba he look righ inta me, yeah. Our mams all da full of happy but da new babys say an do no-ting. We look cross da liddle-big space tween da beds … I see own him an he own see me. Deez liddle babies need no-ting else. So off home we go all packed! An da baby houses side by side la! … an birrday in birrday out … us togedder. An peeplah call me Sinead an call Pig Darren but one day we war playin in da playroom be-an animols on da farm an Darren play da Pig an I play da Runt!

An dat wuz it! An every beddy time our mams pull us away from da odder one. 'Say night to Sinead, Darren.' But Pig jus look ta me an ans (*Snorts an oink.*) An I noel what he mean. So we grow up a bit at a dime an all dat dime we silen when odders roun. No word or no-ting. An wen ten arrive we squeak a diffren way den odders. An da hole a da estate dey talk at us. Look nasty yeah. But me an Pig look stray at dem. An we looka was happenin an we make a whirl where Pig an Runt jar king an queen! Way was goin down in dis clown-town is run by me an Pig fun fun. An Pig look cross at me jus like he look when we were babas an he alla say 'Les kill da town, ya on?' An I alla say – corse I'm on – I'm ja pal, amn't I? An liddle tings we do like robbin an stealin is a good ol feelin, yes indeedy. An we read dem buuks on howta figh da peeplah ya hate. An Pig own has me … an Runt own have him. But we make a whirl dat no one can live sept us two. Bonny an Clyde, ya seen da movie! Fannytastic, yeah! (*Laughs.*) But ya know, we liddle babas no mo. Is all differen. All of a puddin, ders a real big differ-ence.

Sandra is in her late-teens and lives in the Divis flats in West Belfast. She is on a training programme for young offenders on probation or suspended sentence, for joyriding and petty theft. She is bright, tough and a committed cynic. Arthur is another young person on the same programme who has recently been awarded a large compensation sum for injuries received from army gunfire. Their friend, Maureen, was killed a few weeks earlier, trying to protect her joyriding brother who was being pursued by the army. This is Sandra's reply to Arthur's proposal of marriage.

Joyriders *by Christina Reid*

Sandra

The one an' only time I ever wore a white lace frock Arthur, was for my first communion ... an' my mother parades me down the road to get my photo tuk, an' she says to the photographer, 'Isn't our Sandra a picture? Won't she make a beautiful bride?' an' I told her I was never gonna get married, an' she got all dewy-eyed because she thought I wanted to be a nun ... A bride of Christ, or forty years' hard labour ... my mother thinks anything in between is a mortal sin ... She married a big child like you, Arthur, an' what did it get her ... eight kids an' twenty years cookin' cleanin' an' survivin' on grants an' handouts ... You're too like my da fer comfort. Fulla big plans that'll come to nuthin' because yer too soft an' yer too easy-goin' an' havin' all that money won't make ye any different. Whatever your da an' the rest of your ones don't steal from ye, the world will. They'll ate ye alive ... You know what the big trick in this life is? It's knowin' what ye don't want, an' I don't want to be a back-seat joyrider, content to sit and giggle behind the fellas who do the stealin' an' the drivin' ... I stole a car once ... all by myself ... I never told nobody, doin' it was enough ... I just drove it roun' them posh streets in South Belfast until it ran outa petrol, an' then I walked home. Didn't need to boast about it the way the fellas do ... just doin' it was enough ... When the careers' officer come til our school, he asked me what I wanted to do, an' I says, 'I wanna drive roun' in a big car like yer woman outa Bonnie an' Clyde, an' rob banks,' an' he thought I was takin' a hand out him, so I says, 'All right then, I'll settle fer bein' a racin' driver.' An' he says, 'I'd advise you to settle for something less fantastic Sandra' ... They're all the same. They ask ye what ye wanta be, an' then they tell ye what yer allowed to be ... Me wantin' to be a racin' driver is no more fantastical than Maureen believin' the fairy stories ... dilly day-dream, just like her mother before her ... somewhere over the rainbow, bluebirds die ...

Little Lamb's Dublin is one of violence and drug addiction. She has just celebrated her eighteenth birthday at which she was raped by her sister's drug-pushing partner, Shane. Lep – the father of her baby daughter – is a heroin addict. Little Lamb has stolen £500 from her father and is using it to leave Dublin. Here, she is at the airport with her baby daughter, Dove.

Sucking Dublin *by Enda Walsh*

Little Lamb

All of a sudden life's a mad circus!! There's that amount of colour here you could sprinkle it all over a massive trifle and be eatin it for bleedin weeks!! Fuckin rapid, it is!! Deadly!! Hundreds of people settin out for hot spots!! 'Costa Del Fuckin Anywhere But Manky Stinkin Dublin', is a favourite destination!! Thousands of people headin off inta the sun!! All smilin and hoppin up and down like toddlers wantin a piss!! (*Laughs.*) I watch those arrivin back!! Like a bleedin morgue down there in Arrivals!! Worse!! But they're real tanned and sorta continental as they head for the Airport Pub ta mill back the pints!! Numbs the pain of comin back, I suppose!! Well I'm never comin back!! Never!! *Adios Dublin!!* Ya useless fat sweaty bum hole!! I'm fuckin out of here!! 'Whatever ya can give me!!' I said it ta the girl like it was natural! 'There's a cancellation to Majorca, Spain.' 'I'll pay in cash!!' Out with the money!! I think she could smell me feet off the notes, but fuck it, what do I care?! I'm too busy mappin out a new life ta worry about some snotty faced young one!! Ticket in me hand and I can see me on a beach!! The lovely sand and then the sea lappin up on it in the evenin with me as a waitress in a beach-bar servin up cocktails and just listenin ta the sound of Spain!! Me tanned, glowin and all natural! The warm sand squishin up through me toes! What's that funny warmness in your belly, Little Lamb?! That's me feelin happy!! Better get use to it love!! That feelin's stickin around for more than Summer!! I keep thinkin of all that I'm gonna do cause what I gotta do next is so hard and might seem nasty but it has ta be done!! (*Slight pause.*) I take me hands off the pram and leave!! I can sorta hear Dove beginnin ta whinge a bit and I want ta pick her up and give her a hug … kiss my man Lep with that very same hug goodbye … but I'm afraid!! Afraid I'll end up stayin here and never gettin out!! Watch me dream be sucked back inta Dublin! Afraid that I'll end up bringin her and things would be too hard for me!! Too hard for Dove!! Give her a chance, yeah?!! Just walk on!! Leave her for someone ta be a good mammy and daddy!! Might seem fuckin nasty but I gotta be hard!! Have ta be!! Where does softness get me but another helpin of more pain!! I can still feel Steve. Taste his mouth in my mouth. (*Pause.*) Some fat security guard who looks like he hates his job snatches me ticket. (*Pause.*) All I love is gone. But in front I've got me with whatever I want. I spit up the taste of Steve and manky stinkin Dublin. I'm gettin the fuck out of here!

Joanie is a twenty-year-old woman, working as an actor in the Abbey Theatre. Her mother, Mai, is dying of cancer in Jervis Street Hospital in the 1950s. Joanie's childhood has been difficult because of her baby brother's death, her mother's drinking and her parents' vicious arguments. Mai has been given morphine and Joanie appears to her and talks about the environment in which she grew up.

Our Lady of Sligo *by Sebastian Barry*

Joanie

I sang so that the stinking glasses would not be there one morning, perched on the turn of the banisters, or fallen over in the parlour, the little mole-heaps of cigarettes in the stabbed ashtrays. Every morning was solemn as a battlefield with the sad corpses of bottles killed on the scummy carpets and I was like a general sad in the aftermath. All the singing in the world couldn't stop it, though I might burst my breastbone in the singing. *Níl aon tinteán mar do thinteáin féin*, said the teacher, there's no hearth like your own hearth, but she wanted to know why my eyes were black from lack of sleep and when I fell asleep in the hot classroom she was constrained to beat me, bound by the laws governing the mysteries of children to beat me. (...)

Mammy, why did you fold me up in the filthy blankets of the small hours, why did Daddy come in and wake me and send me up the stairs to your bed, him getting into my own warm nest, me just a shard of humanity walking up through the salty moonlight, and the terrible yawp of the attic stairs beyond where the hag of Beare sat in the sucking shadows? And the whale in the bed that was my Mammy, snoring like a man, and those extraordinary farts you made in the cowl of smeared sheets … (...)

… and me slipping in beside you like a salmon into a ruined river. And breathing then with hardship I was, a little engine of distress. And I used to think of the warrior asleep in his stone hut on Knocknarea at the foot of Maeve's gigantic cairn, guarding his queen eternally, and I wondered, was I doing the same? Did every broken mother need a sheltering child? And were you a sort of dark queen like in a story? And in the church where I went to say things to God there were pictures, old oil pictures there were in niches, of Our Lady with her child Jesus, and sometimes it was Our Lady of the Sorrows, and sometimes it was Our Lady of Budapest. And in the end I knew you were Our Lady of Sligo except you had lost your little boy and instead you had the sliver of your tattered girl, a coin of fear and sleeplessness in the palm of your bed.

Maire is a strong, confident woman in her twenties living in Baile Beag, County Donegal, in 1833. She has ten younger siblings and is planning to emigrate to America. The British Army is carrying out an ordnance survey of the whole country. This involves standardising and translating place names from Irish into English. Lieutenant George Yolland is a young officer on his first visit to Ireland. Although Maire can only speak Irish and Yolland can only speak English, they manage to communicate and fall in love. However, Yolland has gone missing and it would appear he has been murdered. Maire goes to the hedge-school where she first met him. She is extremely distressed but attempts to appear calm. Owen is an Irish friend of the officer's and Sarah is a student in the school.

Translations *by Brian Friel*

Maire

He left me home, Owen. And the last thing he said to me – he tried to speak in Irish – he said, 'I'll see you yesterday' – he meant to say 'I'll see you tomorrow.' And I laughed that much he pretended to get cross and he said 'Maypoll! Maypoll!' because I said that word wrong. And off he went, laughing – laughing, Owen! Do you think he's all right? What do *you* think? (...)

He comes from a tiny wee place called Winfarthing. (*She suddenly drops on her hands and knees on the floor – where Owen had his map a few minutes ago – and with her finger traces out an outline map.)* Come here till you see. Look. There's Winfarthing. And there's two other wee villages right beside it; one of them's called Barton Bendish – it's there; and the other's called Saxingham Nethergate – it's about there. And there's Little Walsingham – that's his mother's townland. Aren't they odd names? Sure they make no sense to me at all. And Winfarthing's near a big town called Norwich. And Norwich is in a county called Norfolk. And Norfolk is in the east of England. He drew a map for me on the wet strand and wrote the names on it. I have it all in my head now: Winfarthing – Barton Bendish – Saxingham Nethergate – Little Walsingham – Norwich – Norfolk. Strange sounds, aren't they? But nice sounds; like Jimmy Jack reciting his Homer. (*She gets to her feet and looks around; she is almost serene now. To Sarah)* You were looking lovely last night, Sarah. Is that the dress you got from Boston? Green suits you. (*To Owen)* Something very bad's happened to him, Owen. I know. He wouldn't go away without telling me. Where is he, Owen? You're his friend – where is he? (*Again she looks around the room; then sits on a stool.*) I didn't get a chance to do my geography last night. The master'll be angry with me. (*She rises again.*) I think I'll go home now. The wee ones have to be washed and put to bed and that black calf has to be fed ... My hands are that rough; they're still blistered from the hay. I'm ashamed of them. I hope to God there's no hay to be saved in Brooklyn. (*She stops at the door.*) Did you hear? Nellie Ruadh's baby died in the middle of the night. I must go up to the wake. It didn't last long, did it?

Pax is a sensitive, confused-looking, male, wirehaired terrier — played by a female actor. It is Christmastime and he is in the Mackens' kitchen. They are expecting the arrival of their son, Maurice, and daughter, Terry, who is pregnant by her boyfriend, Benny. All are dreading the Christmas gathering, including Pax. He speaks in a distorted, dog-like manner, echoing the way communication used to be thwarted by media censorship laws in Northern Ireland. Here, he tries to summon his old friend, Rebel, another dog belonging to the family. Rebel has been killed and is roaming the undead animal world.

The Dogs *by Donal O'Kelly*

Pax

Pax! Pax! Pax! That my name. That my doggy name. Nice name. Nice. Like the stuff my mammy put on fish. Fis. She call it fis. Paxo on a piece of fis for my pal Pax. Lovely. I lovely that. Rare. My mammy is a very nice. My fada o-k-too. He a bit big-boom-bom-bom big leda shoe. – Oh – I like to lick the polish off can't help the self – nice mell, get de toe in de mush poor bluggy nose hide it in de liddle gap aside de cooker where he no can get. It a dog's life.

I toth for da many years my name come from the fis-crumb, but one day I learn the no. Watch.

He throws his head back wolf-like and gives a call. Capitals indicate stress.

AilliliuaPEELertrinaCREENacrynaRAPareetheCROP
pyboynaPITCHcapBLACKandtapaRACKrent
CRUCifixionHELLorwalkingGALLowallow
ALlowpuillePUCKaladdieaillilioowowowowoWOW!

Pause while he waits.

Sorry. Sometime the nothing. We try again a minute. My mama nice. My fada okay for de walky or the out for the leak, I can put up with da fuck. And den der Terry. Terry only liddle baba when I first came a liddle pup. We grow dagedder, me de doggy, she de liddle girl. But Terry gone now. All gone wid de Benny fuck. Some melly bedzit, say mama all cry an blow de nose. Lod of cry de late. And lod of fada moan, aboud da bowel an de back. I pud de head in de gap aside of the cooker half od da fucky day. So. That mama, fada, and Terry, and too there was Maurice go away de long time gone. Alway come back wid de shiny point on the shoe, and da smell of da lavender shavy foam.

Da house I alway like. Many room in de fada's mansha. Bright de fron, dark de baci, every de room have a million differ smell. Nigh to just lie a let de waft-waft cross de tip de nose. A ting-tingle, de longa stay, de bedda dey get. Gimme de ereck-reck. I a boy. But de fada-fucka took me da de vet. Only de time I ev ate de steak. Mama gev it doomey after. Sub consummation. Nev ed de meat again. Jus meebe mince no de lumps. Cos de deeth. I no mo de yung turk dog nose. Ah fuck, no mench de turk. Nod dis time de year. Ev Kissma de same. De fuss over de stuffy de bird. Same allway back to Rebel time, he estoll me. Ah, Rebel wait we see if he come now. (*Head back again*)

AilliawilliaSTANDwithinanIrishCOFFinshipspoTATofamineC
APtainBoycottESSexPEELinPITTititiitCROMcruwilliamIReTO
Ntontontonto-theBOWowowilAILLilowowowowoWOW!

Pause while he waits.

Oh-oh. Maybe I no can call 'im back no mo. Me soopernodderel pows are leavin' me. Mebbe I try too hard.

Emily is in her late twenties and has been living in New York for some years. She returns home to Dublin and attends a disastrous, drunken college reunion. Here, she tells the story of her big break as an artist. Later, it is revealed that she has recently discovered she has the AIDS virus.

Digging for Fire *by Declan Hughes*

Emily

Well … ah it's all so corny, it's like Lana Turner on the stool at Schwab's. I'm serving in the café one day, and of course the whole place is like some home for the deluded anyway – no one *really* works there – here's a writer, there's an actress, hello you pair of poets – standard young hopeful stuff. So I'm serving, and this dapper little faggot is really hassling me … (...)

Now I know this guy a little, I don't know who he is, but he knows I paint, and we'd made small talk about the scene before, bitchy stuff mostly. But suddenly he's being really obnoxious, like 'This glass is *not* clean', and 'I don't *believe* this oregano is fresh', and 'I really *need* a raspberry vinaigrette', and so on, and the café is *bunged* so we're all having a ball. Comes to the coffee, he wants a double espresso, decaff., which to me is like having sex with all your clothes on. Anyway, our owner being something of a coffee zealot, there isn't any decaff. on the premises, so he gets an ordinary espresso. Seconds later, these *squeals* suddenly go up, he's shrieking like a stuck pig, 'This is not decaff., this is caffeinated, I wanted decaff.', and I have had it, I stand there 'til he's quietened down, and then I say 'Listen, you big fat baby, why don't you just suck my dick?' (...)

Turns out this guy – Roland Michaels – owns the West 4th Street Gallery. Turns out also he's the kind of queen who keeps Bette Midler in diamonds, he loves a girl with a dirty mouth. I'm cleaning his table, he's left a $20 tip and his card, and written on the back of the card is 'If you paint as tough as you talk, I'm interested. Call me tomorrow.' I called, he saw, he offered. And four months later, I had my first show.

Millie is a thirty-year-old single mother with a five-year-old son. She cannot escape the memory of her teenage years living by Owl Lake. In particular, she is haunted by the final stages of her parents' passionate and tragic relationship. Her father, Robert, is an unreliable and unfaithful husband but her mother, The Mai, is desperately in love with him and unwilling to live without him. Their troubled marriage is ended by The Mai's death, which Millie remembers in this speech.

The Mai *by Marina Carr*

Millie

Maybe we did go into town the following day, I don't remember. It is beyond me now to imagine how we would've spent that day, where we would've gone, what we would've talked about, because when we meet now, which isn't often and always by chance, we shout and roar till we're exhausted or in tears or both, and then crawl away to lick our wounds already gathering venom for the next bout. We usually start with the high language. He'll fling the Fourth Commandment at me, HONOUR THY FATHER! And I'll hiss back, a father has to be honourable before he can be honoured, or some facetious rubbish like that. And we'll pace ourselves like professionals, all the way to the last round, to the language of the gutter, where he'll call me a fuckin' cunt and I'll call him an ignorant bollix! We're well matched, neither ever gives an inch, we can't, it's life and death as we see it. And that's why I cannot remember that excursion into town if it ever occurred. What I do remember, however, is one morning a year and a half later when Robert and I drove into town to buy a blue nightgown and a blue bedjacket for The Mai's waking. Still reeling from the terrible events of that weekend, we walked through The Midland drapery, the floorboards creaking, the other shoppers falling silent and turning away, they knew why we were there and what we'd come for, afraid to look yet needing to see, not wanting to move too closely lest they breathed in the damaged air of Owl Lake that hung about us like a wayward halo. No shroud for The Mai. It was her wish. In one of those throwaway conversations which only become significant with time, The Mai had said she wanted to be buried in blue. So here we were in a daze fingering sky blues, indigo blues, navy blues, lilac blues, night blues, finally settling on a watery blue silk affair. Business done, we moved down the aisle towards the door. A little boy, escaping his mother, ran from the side, banged off Robert and sent him backwards into a display stand. About him on the floor, packets of needles and spools of thread all the colours of the rainbow.

Portia lives with her husband, Raphael, and their three sons in the Belmont Valley in the Midlands. They are financially well-off, but Portia is desperately unhappy and feels suffocated by her family. The source of her extreme unhappiness is her obsessive love for her twin brother, Gabriel, and his death – by drowning in the river – fifteen years ago. On the eve of Portia's thirtieth birthday, the Belmont river throws up a box of keepsakes that had been lost with Gabriel. The day after her birthday, Portia is drawn to the river again. She talks to her sympathetic aunt, Maggie May, about the unique relationship that existed between Gabriel and herself and of her fear that they will not be reunited when she dies.

Portia Coughlan *by Marina Carr*

Portia

Ah'm afraid he won't be there whin ah go. (...)

Afore ah was allas sure, was tha wan thing as kep' me goin'. Now ah don' know anamore, an' yeh ah know thah somewhere he lives an' tha's tha place ah want ta be on'y ah don' know how ta geh there. (...)

Ah chan't help ud, years now, this years ah cuh tha worldt in two, ther's wud Gabriel an' there's withouh Gabriel an' everythin' else ceases be thah division. An' y' ax me abouh Raphael, Raphael don't figure i' my plans, never has, never will. Maggie May ah don' know if anawan realizes whah ud is ta be a twin, everythin's synchronized, tha way ya thinche, tha way ya move, tha way ya speache, tha blinkin' a' yar eyes, tha blood in yar veins moves be unison. Thah time tha cemetary gates fell an Gabriel, tha migh as well've fallen an me too, amimber ah war found unconscious aside of him, wud noh a marche an me, five feeh from wheer tha gahe fell. Tha's on'y a small example of how we ware. Ah'm dead Maggie May, dead an' whah ya seen this long time gone be a ghost who chan't fin' her restin' place, is all. (...)

An' ah knew he war goin' ta do ud. We'd planned ta do ud together an' ah tha las' minuhe ah goh afraid. Stupid! Stupid! An' he jus' wint an in athouh me an' ah challed him bache an' he didn' hare me an account a' tha swell an' jus' kep' an wadin' in an' ah'm standin' an tha banche shoutin' ah him ta chome bache an' ah tha las second he turns thinkin' ah'm ahind him an' he sees me standin'. Hees face Maggie May, tha looche an hees face an' ah'm roarin' buh no soun' is chomin' ouh an' he tries ta mache tha banche buh th'undertow do have him an' a wave washes over him an' he's gone wud our box a' things ... jus' liche thah ... Don't tell Mother thah so ya wont Maggie May, nor Daddy, for tha hahe me enough as ud is.

Deborah is thirty-three and has attempted a number of different careers. She is currently trying to break into photography. Her older sister, Mary, is a travel agent who has recently been left widowed with children. The relationship between Deborah and Mary has been troubled since their mother died in a car accident when they were girls. Deborah has brought Mary camping – to the scene of their mother's death – in the hope that they can work through their problems. Here, Deborah relives the moment their mother died.

New Morning *by Declan Hughes*

Deborah

It was *not* sunny, it was … *flecked* … (...)

Storm-flecked … a hill-top in clear sunlight here, rain in a valley there, the road gloomy with grey cloud. Shifting all the time though, rain and sun and cloud changing places like … fickle partners at some wild dance. (...)

And we four safe in the Red Zephyr … the nearest Daddy could come to a Pink Cadillac … cruising along out to … see the waterfall? Visit a castle? While away the holiday morning somehow. Out for a spin, that's what we were. Out for a bit of an old spin. Stopping for treats, Cidona and crisps, and the pub stiff and yawny and smelling of last night's smoke, and breath and beer – and then off again … singing, 'cause there's no radio … 'Long Black Limousine' … 'In the Ghetto'…

(*Sings*) If I can dream … of a warmer sun
Where hope keeps shining on everyone
Tell me why, oh why, oh why won't that sun appear? (...)

And then we slow down to play Driving in the Dark. You with your hands over Daddy's eyes, and the both of us screaming, and then silent … *this carry-on will end in tears, Miss Madam* … slowly slowly up the hill … not a waver, not so much as a swerve … *I wish you'd stop this love, the road's too narrow, it's dangerous* … red nails glint in the light as her hands grip the wooden dashboard, knuckles clenched white against the stain … *I have opened my mouth unto the Lord, and cannot go back* … hill's taking for ever to climb, what's at the top? What's at the top? Sky's at the top, sky road with the view, but the road's getting very narrow and windy … maybe we *should* stop … Keep going, you can do it, don't listen to them, careful now, careful … *Oh Jesus we're going over* … Turn right, *sharp* right, *sharper* … *Take your hands off his eyes you stupid bitch* …

Pause

The door flew open when we swerved away from the edge. I was screaming, eyes clamped tight. When I opened them, she was gone.

Lily Matthews dies in 1974 at the age of seventy-four. She has been a staunch Protestant all her life and her ghost is affronted to find her Belfast home now occupied by a young, separated Catholic woman, Marion. Marion is fascinated by the details of Lily's past and, in this scene, she confronts the ghost of Lily's thirty-three-year-old self about the affair she had in the early 1930s with her lodger, Alan Ferris. Lily had a child by Alan when her husband, Alfie, was away. She abandoned the baby on the steps of a Baptist Church in order to keep it a secret from Alfie.

Pentecost *by Stewart Parker*

Lily

My Alfie would have struck the pair of us down dead. He was capable of it, he knew it too, he told me the day we moved in here, never make me lose my temper … he never found out, about the child, that was the one mercy, he was away for that whole year tramping all over England, looking for work with Jackie Midgely. Nobody ever knew but me, my own mother was dead by then with the T.B., I was inclined towards stoutness then anyway … one day it just arrived … on that floor, five hours I lay there … I delivered it myself. By the time Alfie come home again, the whole thing was over and done, as though it had never been … he had no inkling of any of it, from then till his dying day. (...)

Oh, sweet God in heaven forgive me! (...)

I sinned against my own flesh in lust and fornication, I had to desert my own baby, nobody ever knew only the Lord our God knew and His eye was on me all right, burning into the very soul of me, He alone was witness to the torment that I've suffered every living hour in this house where the very walls and doors cry out against me, there was never anybody to tell the knife that went through me a dozen dozen times a day, minding how I left my child, walking away from him, leaving him bundled up there in that wooden box, nobody to help me, only me here in this house, gnawing and tearing away at my own heart and lights, day in day out … until I was all consumed by my own wickedness, on the inside, nothing left but the shell of me, for appearance's sake … still and all. At least I never let myself down – never cracked. Never surrendered. Not one inch. I went to my grave a respectable woman, Mrs Alfred George Matthews, I never betrayed him. That was the way I atoned, you see. I done him proud. He never knew any reason to be ashamed of me, or doubt my loyalty. From the day we met till the day I went to my grave.

Valerie is a woman in her thirties who has just left her husband, Daniel, in Dublin and moved to the North-West of Ireland. Her daughter, Niamh, died in a swimming accident the previous year. Valerie spends an evening in a small rural bar, meeting some of her new neighbours. Ghost stories are exchanged. This gives Valerie the courage to talk about her daughter's fear of the dark and to share with the local men an experience she had a few months after Niamh's death.

The Weir *by Conor McPherson*

Valerie

But I mean, she used to be even be scared that when she got up in the morning that Mammy and Daddy would have gone away and she'd be in the house on her own. That was one she told Daniel's mother. And all the furniture and carpets and everything would be gone. I mean, you know? So I told her after that, you know, we'd never, you know, it was ridiculous. And that if she was scared or worried at all during the day to ring me, and I'd come and get her, and there was nothing to worry about. And she knew our number, she was very good at learning numbers off and everything. She knew ours and her nana's and mine at work. She knew them all.

But then, in March, last year, the school had a, a sponsored swim, and the kids were going to swim a length of the pool. And I promised I was going to go and watch her. But I got ... I was late, out of work, and I was only going to be in time to meet her afterwards, but em, when I got there ... There was an ambulance and I thought, like, the pool is in the Central Remedial Clinic, so I thought like it was just somebody being dropped there. I didn't really pay any attention.

But when I got in, I saw that there was no one in the pool and one of the teachers was there with a group of kids. And she was crying and some of the children were crying. And this woman, another one of the mums came over and said there'd been an accident. And Niamh had hit her head in the pool and she'd been in the water and they had been trying to resuscitate her. But she said she was going to be alright. And I didn't believe it was happening. I thought it must have been someone else. And I went into, I was brought into, a room and Niamh was on a table. It was a table for table-tennis, and an ambulance man was giving her the ... kiss of life.

She was in her bathing suit. And the ambulance man said he didn't think that what he was doing was working. And he didn't know if she was alive. And he wrapped her in a towel and carried her out to the ambulance. And I got in the back with him. And they radioed on ahead, they were going to put her on a machine in Beaumont and try to revive her there. But the ambulance man knew, I think. She wasn't breathing, and he just knew and he said if I wanted to just say goodbye to her in the ambulance in case I didn't get a chance in the hospital.

And I gave her a little hug. She was freezing cold. And I told her Mammy loved her very much. She just looked asleep but her lips were gone blue and she was dead.

And it had happened so fast. Just a few minutes. And I don't think I have to tell you. How hard it was. Between me and Daniel, as well. It didn't seem real. At the funeral I just thought I could go and lift her out of the coffin and that would be the end of all this.

I think Daniel was. I don't know if he actually, blamed me, there was nothing I could do. But he became very busy in his work. Just. Keeping himself … em. But I was, you know, I was more, just I didn't really know what I was doing. Just walking around or sitting in the house, with Daniel's mother, fussing around the place.

Just, months of this. Not really talking about it, like.

Pause.

But, and then one morning. I was in bed, Daniel had gone to work. I usually lay there for a few hours, trying to stay asleep, really, I suppose. And the phone rang. And I just left it. I wasn't going to get it. And it rang for a long time. Em, eventually it stopped, and I was dropping off again. But then it started ringing again, for a long time. So I thought it must have been Daniel trying to get me. Someone who knew I was there.

So I went down and answered it. And. The line was very faint. It was like a crossed line. There were voices, but I couldn't hear what they were saying. And then I heard Niamh. She said, 'Mammy?' And I … just said, you know? 'Yes?' And she said … she wanted me to come and collect her.

I mean, I wasn't sure whether this was a dream or her leaving us had been a dream. I just said 'Where are you?'

And she said she thought she was at Nana's. In the bedroom. But Nana wasn't there. And she was scared. There were children knocking in the walls and the man was standing across the road, and he was looking up and he was going to cross the road. And could I come and get her?

And I said I would, of course I would. And I dropped the phone and I ran out to the car in just a tee-shirt I slept in. And I drove to Daniel's mother's house. And I could hardly see, I was crying so much. I mean, I knew she wasn't going to be there. I knew she was gone. But to think wherever she was … that … And there was nothing I could do about it. Daniel's mother had to get a doctor and I … slept for a day or two. But it was … Daniel felt that I … needed to face up to Niamh being gone. But I just thought he should face up to what happened to me. He was insisting I got some 'treatment' and then … everything would be okay. But you know, what can help that, if she's out there? She still … she still needs me.

Maureen has been in Mountjoy Jail for shoplifting and has been addicted to heroin. In the past, her brother-in-law, Eddie, has been unwilling for his family to associate with her. However, he is now a heroin addict himself and has lost his wife and daughter as a result. He has come to Maureen to find out where he can get a fix. He threatens to kill her if she does not tell him.

One Last White Horse *by Dermot Bolger*

Maureen

No you won't. You haven't got the guts, lover boy. You'd have to look me in the eye to do it. And you've never bothered looking at me once, have you? Have you ever asked how I feel, Mr Fucking Perfect? Do you even know the names of my children? (...)

I want you to see me, to lift your head and finally acknowledge that I am here. I have lived, I had a family and a house too. First year on the scuttery estate in Balbriggan they had a community week with a bonfire and a monster sing-song. Everybody sitting looking at each other until they started singing the jingles from the ads on television. God, I laughed so much ... (*her voice drops)* he hit me when we got inside the door. Four years and two kids and I'm only having my twenty-first. We couldn't even have it in the city centre. No, the Grand Hotel on the Main Street, chicken and chips and gawking at the faces from across the road. I drank so much I went walkabout on my way to the ladies, woke up in some fisherman's bed, the middle of the night, the police outside and my husband banging on the door. The fisherman was kneeling up naked, peering out the blinds. I could see how I'd clawed the skin off his back when I came. Four years of my youth to make up in one night. Gerard kept the house and kids, I wasn't thinking much, just wanted time away. He did it all legal like a proper bank clerk, I was signing things I'd only half read. Six months of freedom, I figured, and I'd go back to poxy little Gerard for the kids. Six weeks later I got his postcard with their new address in Canada. (...)

You listen good. Losing your kids, it's like having the heart torn from you. I was tainted goods at twenty-one. Amazing how men can sense it in a night-club, like they were doing you a big favour letting you suck on their dick. I lost everything to a bastard doing his duty, just looking for an excuse to get away from me. You had a wife and a kid who loved you, you had a home and you just blew it all.

Karen is a thirty-five-year-old woman from Derry who has just returned home from her daughter's wedding. Karen's husband, Declan, is a member of the IRA and has been in prison for the past nine years. She visits him every Thursday. In this speech, she talks about the visit just over a week ago, when she brought her pregnant daughter with her to tell Declan about the wedding.

Twinkletoes *by Jennifer Johnston*

Karen

Anyway the long and short of it was that I made her take the day off and she came up in the bus with me.

He was so glad to see her.

He looked great, all dressed up and his face excited with this big smile ...

I kept my fingers crossed.

He held her hand so tight, like he thought she might fly away.

You're so pretty, just like your mammy.

I sat watching them, quietly, thinking my own thoughts.

And the time flew in and she never said what she'd come to say.

So, out of my silence, I said, Haven't you something to tell your daddy?

She stopped talking and looked at the table.

She gave a little nervous clear to her throat.

I'm getting married on Saturday week.

He didn't seem to take it in.

So I repeated what she'd said.

But you're only a kid, he said.

I'm seventeen.

You're only left school. You're too young.

You and mammy were going out when she was only seventeen, she told me that.

He glared at me.

Karen ... he said.

I shook my head.

She won't listen, I said.

She'll listen to me. Won't you listen, love? You're only young. You've all your life in front of you.

I'm getting married on Saturday week no matter what you say and that's all there is to it.

She stood up, ready to go.

At least tell your daddy what his name is.

Declan. Isn't that funny. Same as you. O'Hare.

He looked like someone had hit him.

Why didn't you tell me before Karen?

I could only shake my head.

He's a nice lad, I whispered.

He looked like he'd looked in the court the day the judge had said he was going away.

I'd like to meet him, he said.

Sentences to run concurrently the judge said.

After the wedding. I'll bring him up some Thursday after the wedding.

Three life sentences to run concurrently.

If you gave a cat three life sentences, it would still have six lives left.

Or eight if they ran concurrently.

And they don't run, believe you me.

They crawl.

You might have waited till I came out, he said.

Thanks, she said. We've better things to do with our lives than wait for miracles to happen.

She turned and walked out.

She didn't kiss him or nothing.

Young people can be ... can be ...

I've done my best, I said. Honest to God, Declan ... very hard sometimes. Yes.

I know, love.

He smiled at me.

My dad's helping out with the wedding. We'll do it well. You know, the hotel, a meal, a few drinks.

Have a band, he said.

Yes.

Tell me Karen ... is she ... is she ...

No, I lied.

He believed me. I could see him believing me.
I'm quite good at lying.
Thirty-five.
I want to dance.
Jive.
Jitterbug.
Tango.
Rock.
I really want to rock.
I want to have more kids.
I want to love.
Not just on Thursdays.
Aye, Declan, I love you.
I lie well.
You've fucking well ruined my life, Declan. That's what I want to say.
And your own.
You're a hero.
Wear it well, I say.
I'm just a woman whose plastic shoes hurt.

Lizzie Finn is an Irishwoman working as a dancer in an English music-hall in the 1890s. She is a strong, good-looking woman in her mid/late-thirties. In the audience one night is Robert, an Irish gentleman whom Lizzie has met once by accident. When he sees Lizzie on stage dancing the can-can, he leaps forward and tries to cover her revealing costume with his coat. She feels he has shamed her and afterwards, in her dressing room with her dancing partner, Jelly Jane, she explains the reason for her outrage.

The Only True History of Lizzie Finn
by Sebastian Barry

Lizzie

I don't like a person to put shame to me. (*After a little*.) My mother went barefoot all her life, but the roads were green all over Corcaguiney then, if there were roads. There used to be a saying about the roads of Corcaguiney, as being things that did not exist. They might say a particular person's virtue was like the roads of Corcaguiney – you know? (...)

But in our time there were roads enough, to carry my father and his singing voice about the place. He knew songs from the islands that he didn't sing much, unless we were rowed over to the Blasket on a sweet summer day. He knew trademen's songs and tinkers' songs and he knew little parts out of operettas that he could sing for the rich people if he were asked. He liked to sing for the rich because he had a great love of fine chairs and carpets and plates – he liked to look at them in the rooms. But then he'd be as happy to go out on the frosty road again, and be gone, the three of us, be a memory, a memory of singing. And he knew that the people all over Corcaguiney would be humming his tunes about the hills if they wandered there, or about the strands, or in their houses. He was the very singing soul of Corcaguiney. He never let shame be put to us. Singing or dancing to him were the highest things a person could put himself to. And he always said the very heart of a person was revealed in their singing. You could take a dairymaid out of a byre, and set her in the shitty yard, and if she could sing, all paradise and Beulah would appear about her and the listeners would be transported there and then. He took fever from a hungry ditch and my mother followed after him. I will never forget him or dishonour his memory, that singing man. For a man with a singing voice like that is God, or the shadow of God on this earth. And I am the daughter forever of that singing man.

Angela lives in Wexford town with her husband, Donal, and their children. She begins having an affair with Artie, the sacristan of the local church where she arranges flowers. Their illicit meetings take place in the belfry.

Belfry *by Billy Roche*

Angela

The heart's its own boss Artie I think. People can give their love away as freely as they want but not the heart. The heart's its own boss boy!

I have a photo at home yeh know that keeps turnin' up to kind of haunt me all the time. I'll find it in a drawer or somewhere or down in the end of my handbag when I'm rootin' around for my keys. No idea how it got there! … It was taken on the steps of White's Hotel. Donal's mother and father's fiftieth anniversary it was. We had a bit of a do for them. All the lads came home from England and all for it. This was supposed to be a picture of just the immediate family so I stepped back into the hotel doorway out of the way. It had been snowin' and the steps leadin' up to the hotel were still covered in slush. I think the photographer must have had a few drinks in him or somethin' because when it came out you could see me as clear as day standin' in the background. I looked like a little orphan standin' there in the cold. Everybody laughed when they saw it. It was as if I didn't belong in Donal's life at all. You'd swear I was tryin' to sneak my way into it or somethin'. Or out of it, whichever the case may be. It's a great photograph though. I'm not coddin' yeh, you can nearly hear them all laughin' in it …

She chuckles and goes behind the raised lid of the basket, out of sight.

Our Maude says that there's only two real choices open to people in life yeh know. Whether to tap the good side of them or the bad side. If yeh tap the good side then all you'll see is the good in people and the good in everything and you'll be happy. If yeh tap the bad side of yeh then you'll be devious and snakey and bad and you'll never be really contented. Everytime I look at that photograph I keep thinkin' how contented they all look and I keep wonderin' why I'm not in there with them … (*She emerges, wearing only an altar boy's surplus.*) Do yeh think I've tapped the bad side of me Artie? (...)

Huh? This is about the length of the dresses that meself and Maude used to wear now when we'd be goin' off to the dances. Me poor Da used to nearly do his nut. 'There's no point in havin' nice legs Daddy if you're not prepared to show them off,' we'd say to him … What do yeh think?

Belfry *is the third play in* The Wexford Trilogy.

Maggie is a fun-loving, thirty-eight year old woman. She is the second eldest of the five Mundy sisters living together near the County Donegal village of Ballybeg in 1936. Money is scarce and Maggie herself generates no income but keeps house for the rest of the family. Her sister, Kate, comes back from the village, having just met Bernie O'Donnell who is home for the first time in twenty years with her twin daughters. The mention of her name evokes this memory from Maggie.

Dancing at Lughnasa *by Brian Friel*

Maggie

When I was sixteen I remember slipping out one Sunday night – it was this time of year, the beginning of August – and Bernie and I met at the gate of the workhouse and the pair of us off to a dance in Ardstraw. I was being pestered by a fellow called Tim Carlin at the time but it was really Brian McGuinness that I was – that I was keen on. Remember Brian with the white hands and the longest eyelashes you ever saw? But of course he was crazy about Bernie. Anyhow the two boys took us on the bar of their bikes and off the four of us headed to Ardstraw, fifteen miles each way. If Daddy had known, may he rest in peace …

And at the end of the night there was a competition for the Best Military Two-step. And it was down to three couples: the local pair from Ardstraw; wee Timmy and myself – he was up to there on me; and Brian and Bernie …

And they were just so beautiful together, so stylish; you couldn't take your eyes off them. People just stopped dancing and gazed at them …

And when the judges announced the winners – they were probably blind drunk – naturally the local couple came first; and Timmy and myself came second; and Brian and Bernie came third.

Poor Bernie was stunned. She couldn't believe it. Couldn't talk. Wouldn't speak to any of us for the rest of the night. Wouldn't even cycle home with us. She was right, too: they should have won; they were just so beautiful together …

And that's the last time I saw Brian McGuinness – remember Brian with the …? And the next thing I heard he had left for Australia …

She was right to be angry, Bernie. I know it wasn't fair – it wasn't fair at all. I mean they must have been blind drunk, those judges, whoever they were …

Dolly is thirty-nine. Her husband, Stephen, works in England, while she is left to bring up their children. She is promiscuous with various men in the area and is now heavily pregnant by one of them. In the past, she has cared for her bedridden grandmother, Mommo, but Dolly's sister, Mary, has now taken on that onerous task. Dolly visits her sister and grandmother late one Sunday evening, proposing that Mary take the baby when it is born. Accusations and recriminations escalate as the sisters argue over who has had the toughest life.

Bailegangaire *by Tom Murphy*

Dolly

No! No! You had it easy! – You had it – You had – I had – I had ten! – I had a lifetime! – A lifetime! – Here with herself, doin' her every bidding, listenin' to her seafóid (*rambling*) gettin' worse till I didn't know where I was! – Pissin' in the bed beside me – I had a lifetime! Then the great Stephen – the surprise of it! comes coortin'! Never once felt any – real – warmth from him – what's wrong with him? – but he's my rescuer, my saviour. But then, no rhyme or reason to it – He could've got a job at that plant, but he couldn't wait to be gone either! Then waitin' for the hero, my rescuer, the sun shining out of his eighty-five-pounds-a-week arse, to come home at Christmas. No interest in me – oh, he used me! – or in the children, or the rotten thatch or the broken window, or Conor above moving in his fence from *this* side. I'm fightin' all the battles. Still fightin' the battles. And what d'yeh think he's doin' now this minute? Sittin' by the hearth in Coventry, is he? Last Christmas an' he was hardly off the bus, Old Sharp Eyes whisperin' into his ear about me. Oooo, but he waited. Jesus, how I hate him! Jesus, how I hate them! Men! Had his fun and games with me that night, *and* first thing in the morning. Even sat down to eat the hearty breakfast I made. Me thinkin', still no warmth, but maybe it's goin' to be okay. Oooo, but I should've known from *experience* about-the-great-up-standin'-Steph-en-evrabody's-fav-our-ite.

Because, next thing he has me by the hair of the head, fistin' me down in the mouth. Old Sharp Eyes there, noddin' her head every time he struck an' struck an' kicked an' kicked an' pulled me round the house by the hair of the head. Jesus, men! (*Indicating the outdoors where she had her sex.*) You-think-I-enjoy? I-use-*them* ! Jesus, hypocrisy! An' then, me left with my face like a balloon – you saw a lot of me last Christmas' didn't yeh? – my body black and blue, the street angel an' his religious mother – 'As true as Our Lady is in heaven now, darlin's' – over the road to visit you an' Mommo with a little present an' a happy an' a holy Christmas now darlin's an' blessed St-fuckin'-Jude an' all the rest of them flyin' about for themselves up there.

Maureen is a plain, single woman of forty who has spent some time in an English psychiatric hospital. She lives in a small town in Connemara, where she takes care of her manipulative mother, Mag. Mag has destroyed a vital letter in an effort to thwart Maureen's chance of a loving relationship with Pato. However, Maureen found this out just before Pato was due to leave for America. Here, she tells how her reunion with him went – an encounter that is later revealed to be a figment of Maureen's imagination. At the end of the speech, we discover that Mag – the recipient of the speech – has been murdered by Maureen.

The Beauty Queen of Leenane

by Martin McDonagh

Maureen

To Boston. To Boston I'll be going. Isn't that where them two were from, the Kennedys, or was that somewhere else, now? Robert Kennedy I did prefer over Jack Kennedy. He seemed to be nicer to women. Although I haven't read up on it. (*Pause.*) Boston. It does have a nice ring to it. Better than England it'll be, I'm sure. Although where wouldn't be better than England? No shite I'll be cleaning there, anyways, and no names called, and Pato'll be there to have a say-so anyways if there was to be names called, but I'm sure there won't be. The Yanks do love the

Irish. (*Pause.*) Almost begged me, Pato did. Almost on his hands and knees, he was, near enough crying. At the station I caught him, not five minutes to spare, thanks to you. Thanks to your oul interfering. But too late to be interfering you are now. Oh aye. Be far too late, although you did give it a good go, I'll say that for you. Another five minutes and you'd have had it. Poor you. Poor selfish oul bitch, oul you. (*Pause.*) Kissed the face off me, he did, when he saw me there. Them blue eyes of his. Them muscles. Them arms wrapping me. 'Why did you not answer me letter?' And all for coming over and giving you a good kick he was when I told him, but 'Ah no,' I said, 'isn't she just a feeble-minded oul feck, not worth dirtying your boots on?' I was defending you there. (*Pause.*) 'You will come to Boston with me so, me love, when you get up the money.' 'I will, Pato. Be it married or be it living in sin, what do I care? What do I care if tongues'd be wagging? Tongues have wagged about me before, let them wag again. Let them never stop wagging, so long as I'm with you, Pato, what do I care about tongues? So long as it's you and me, and the warmth of us cuddled up, and the skins of us asleep, is all I ever really wanted anyway.' (*Pause.*) 'Except we do still have a problem, what to do with your oul mam, there,' he said. 'Would an oul folks home be too harsh?' 'It wouldn't be too harsh but it would be too expensive.' 'What about your sisters so?' 'Me sisters wouldn't have the bitch. Not even a half-day at Christmas to be with her can them two stand. They clear forgot her birthday this year as well as that. 'How do you stick her without going off your rocker?' they do say to me. Behind her back, like. (*Pause.*) 'I'll leave it up to yourself so,' Pato says. He was on the train be this time, we was kissing out the window, like they do in films. 'I'll leave it up to yourself so, whatever you decide. If it takes a month, let it take a month. And if it's finally you decide you can't bear to be parted from her and have to stay behind, well, I can't say I would like it, but I'd understand. But if even a year it has to take for you to decide, it is a year I will be waiting, and won't be minding the wait.' 'It won't be a year it is you'll be waiting, Pato,' I called out then, the train was pulling away. 'It won't be a year nor yet nearly a year. It won't be a week!'

Molly Sweeney lost her sight at the age of ten months and has now been blind for forty years. An opportunity arises for Molly to regain her sight and she is urged by her husband, Frank, and the surgeon, Mr Rice, to grasp it. To Frank, Molly represents another good cause for which he can fight; to Mr Rice, she represents a chance to restore his professional reputation. Molly works in a health club and has made a full life for herself in darkness but decides to undergo the operation.

Molly Sweeney *by Brian Friel*

Molly

I don't know what I expected when the bandages would be removed. I think maybe I didn't allow myself any expectations. I knew that in his heart Frank believed that somehow, miraculously, I would be given the perfect vision that sighted people have, even though Mr Rice had told us again and again that my eyes weren't capable of that vision. And I knew what Mr Rice hoped for: that I would have partial sight. 'That would be a total success for me' is what he said. But I'm sure he meant it would be great for all of us.

As for myself, if I had any hope, I suppose it was that neither Frank nor Mr Rice would be too disappointed because it had all become so important for them.

No, that's not accurate either. Yes, I did want to see. For God's sake of course I wanted to see. But that wasn't an expectation, not even a mad hope. If there was a phantom desire, a fantasy in my head, it was this. That perhaps by some means I might be afforded a brief excursion to this land of vision; not to live there – just to visit. And during my stay to devour it again and again and again with greedy, ravenous eyes. To gorge on all those luminous sights and wonderful spectacles until I knew every detail intimately and utterly – every ocean, every leaf, every field, every star, every tiny flower. And then, oh yes, then to return home to my own world with all that rare understanding within me forever.

No, that wasn't even a phantom desire. Just a stupid fantasy. And it came into my head again when that poor nurse was trying to prettify me for Mr Rice. And I thought to myself: It's like being back at school – I'm getting dressed up for the annual excursion.

When Mr Rice did arrive, even before he touched me, I knew by his quick, shallow breathing that he was far more nervous than I was. And then as he took off the bandages his hands trembled and fumbled.

'There we are,' he said. 'All off. How does that feel?'

'Fine,' I said. Even though I felt nothing. Were all the bandages off?

'Now, Molly. In your own time. Tell me what you see.'

Nothing. Nothing at all. Then out of the void a blur; a haze; a body of mist; a confusion of light, colour, movement. It had no meaning.

'Well?' he said. 'Anything? Anything at all?'

I thought: Don't panic; a voice comes from a face; that blur is his face; look at him.

'Well? Anything?'

Something moving; large; white; the nurse? And lines, black lines, vertical lines. The bed? The door?

'Anything, Molly?' A bright light that hurt. The window maybe?

'I'm holding my hand before your eyes, Molly. Can you see it?'

A reddish blob in front of my face; rotating; liquefying; pulsating. Keep calm. Concentrate.

'Can you see my hand, Molly?'

'I think so … I'm not sure …'

'Now I'm moving my hand slowly.'

'Yes … yes …'

'Do you see my hand moving?'

'Yes …'

'What way is it moving?'

'Yes … I do see it … up and down … up and down … Yes! I see it! I do! Yes! Moving up and down! Yes-yes-yes!'

'Splendid!' he said. 'Absolutely splendid! You are a clever lady!'

And there was such delight in his voice. And my head was suddenly giddy. And I thought for a moment – for a moment I thought I was going to faint.

Stella is a timid, forty-three-year-old woman, habitually downtrodden by her astronomy-obsessed husband, Dermot. Together with their teenage daughter, Tara, they have recently moved to a house in the Wicklow hills where Dermot is looking forward to photographing a comet colliding with Jupiter. Stella has had a particularly chaotic evening as she tries to please her husband by wearing contact lenses rather than glasses and tries to help Paul and Geraldine – two friends with marital problems of their own who have come to visit. She has been left alone for a moment as Dermot goes off to bury a dog he has accidentally killed and gives vent to her pent-up frustrations.

Stella by Starlight *by Bernard Farrell*

Stella

(*Furiously to herself*) Jupiter! Do you ever think about anything else, do you? And you don't want my contact lenses in, do you not? Right. Right. Fine. Out they come – suits me, I never wanted the bloody things anyway. (*Takes out her contact lenses and flings them across the room*) And you don't like my glasses, do you not? Well tough – *I* like them and I'm going to bloody-well wear them, even when I'm sleeping I'll wear them! (*Puts on her glasses*) But don't touch your telescope or your bloody computer or say a bad word about that mad-man Harold. And you want me to kick Geraldine out into the night? – well you can forget that! (*To the sliding door*) And you, Paul, you can forget it too; you and your Japanese Four-Ball and your little hotel in Kildare and the little bastards snapping at your heels. (*Angrily pours a drink*) Well who cares? – not me because I have had enough! And I'll say this to your faces, word for word, I'll scream it at all of you. (*Stops. Then wearily*) Except, of course, I won't, because all I can ever do is apologise. Forty-three years of age and I'm still apologising to everybody. I can see it all now: one day I'll finish up sitting here apologising to the sheep and goats ... (*Sleepily, goes to the settee*) ... telling them about Tara gone off to college, Dermot in looking at the stars and doing his Open University Course and me, still here, living out what's left of my life, apologising ... and the sheep and goats will all look at me, with their big dopey eyes, and they'll all say ... (*Drowsily*) ... 'And who's to blame for that?'

Lil Sweeney lives in the Maria Goretti Mansions – a block of flats in Dublin. A little over a year ago, her daughter, Chrissie, died of Aids – a common cause of death in the flats. Her husband has become withdrawn, spending most of the time with his pigeons. Lil's home has just been broken into by some young thugs. Lil replaces various photographs of Chrissie on the mantelpiece. She is manically exact about returning each one to the position it occupied before the break-in. As she does so, she talks to her dead daughter.

Mrs Sweeney *by Paula Meehan*

Lil

You're better off dead, Chrissie. Ah now don't be looking at me with your big sad eyes. I don't mean that. I don't mean that at all. I didn't even get a chance to clock who they were. They were on top of me before I knew it. What am I going to do Chrissie? Look at it. Just look at it. Could be worse. I could've been here.

She finds this hilarious.

Do you hear me Chrissie? I'd've slit them belly to neck and gutted them. The little shites. And where was your Da? That's what I'd like to know. Where was he, Chrissie? Oweny Burke was saying the other night ... What was he saying? That the dead are all around us, looking out for us. Keeping an eye. You're falling down badly on the job Chrissie. Or maybe you're doing a grand job. We could've been murdered alive in our beds.

She goes to window.

Four times. Four times this month Chrissie. Well I'm not putting glass in it again. They'd rob the eyes from your head if you didn't blink now and then.

She fetches a couple of sheets of plywood and hammer, picks sheet nearest in size to smashed pane of glass, balances plastic milk crate on chair, climbs up precariously and begins to hammer wood to window frame.

And did you see what they took Chrissie? Eh? One radio alarm clock (*Hammer*) one Magimix blender (*Hammer*) the remote control to go with the telly they robbed the last time (*Hammer*) me new coat (*Hammer*) me snaky earrings (*Hammer*) Sweeney's drill (*Hammer*) Sweeney's leather jacket (*Hammer*) Sweeney's Trophy, his shaggin trophy with the golden pigeon on it, Leinster Champion 1989. King of the Fanciers. Ugly fucking yoke. King of the Avoiders would be more like. Head in the Sand Award. Eyes closed and up to the neck in shite award. Creek with no paddle award. (*Sings*) 'O where are you now when we need you, Da da da da da da da dee, Da da da da da da da da da, And only our livers are free.' (*Hammer*) Not much for their trouble, hardly worth the effort, Chrissie. Now if they'd any sense they would have waited until we'd built up a few more bits and pieces. Left us a couple of months, at least until we replaced the telly and the vid, maybe a CD player, make it worth their while. Rule number one – don't hit the same flat too often. Flat Breaking for Beginners: wait until the inmates have got over the shock of the last break in. Just when they're breathing normally again and their hearts have stopped hammering at the slightest noise in the night, and they are lulled completely into a false sense of security – then – strike! Robber's Etiquette: do not shit in the bed, do not smear excrement on the kitchen walls, do not piss in the wardrobe. (*She begins to weep*) Jesus Chrissie. (*Hammers last nail in and closes window. Sudden silence. She climbs down and surveys her work*) They took the curtains. Curious that. What would they get for a set of old curtains and a few nets? Are their minds gone with the drugs? If it *was* the junkies. Was it Chrissie? Old pals of yours up to their junky tricks, eh? What they got here wouldn't fix them up for a day. You'd think they'd go out to Howth or Rathgar or … Sure they wouldn't even have the energy to get the bus out. This was the work of kids. For the hell of it. On their own people, but! Preying on their own people like animals. No. Animals is too good for them. Vampires. Ha! Blood from stones. Blood from fucking stones.

Lizzie is a Catholic woman who fell in love with Jack Boles – a Protestant man. They married and moved from Leitrim to Fermanagh, but the legacy of hatred and vengeance followed them to their new home. Jack was murdered by Frank Beirne – a violent Catholic man who had wanted Lizzie to be his wife. Lizzie is talking to her daughter, Sarah, and she remembers the day her husband was killed.

At the Black Pig's Dyke *by Vincent Woods*

Lizzie

Frank Beirne …

He wanted me. He always wanted me and I was soft with him at the start because I was afraid and because he was handsome enough. He'd catch hold of me any chance he got and grip me so hard I'd bruise from the dent of pressure. That was the song he used to sing whenever he saw me – and it was like a knife pointin' at yer throat.

It was August it happened. Jack went out as usual that mornin' to the hayfield. It was a late summer that year and the big meadow was still down. The child was out playin' and before I knew it the clock was strikin' noon. I prepared his bit of lunch and I didn't put too much wonder in his not comin' for it – I thought he must be workin' on while the weather held up.

It held till three and the sky opened then with rain that would rival the flood. I thought , 'He'll be in any minute now,' but he didn't come. So I thought, 'he's shelterin' in the old pighouse and he'll be down as soon as it stops.' It stopped about half past four and I sat waitin' for him to come in. I sat for an hour and I knew then there was something terrible wrong. I took Sarah by the hand and we walked up the hill to where he was workin'.

I didn't find him straight away. I walked the length and breadth of the meadow and called, 'Jack, Jack – where are ye?' There was no answer – only the echo of my own voice comin' back from the outhouses ... I walked up the lane towards them same buildings. There was a bush of redcurrants just before you turned in on the flags and I stopped and took a fistful for Sarah. I don't know why I did.

He was lyin' in a puddle of water outside the byre door – his face from me – and the water near as red as the berries on her lips. He'd been stuck in the neck like a pig; and his hands – his hands that played the melodeon – were slashed to ribbons like he'd tried to ward off the blows of a knife.

Dead for certain. Dead and no cure. Jack Boles that I ran away with. Jack Boles that I lay with the night of the fools' weddin'. Jack Boles my husband ...

Maela, a woman in her forties, has refused to accept the death of her daughter. She is in a Derry graveyard with a group of people waiting for the dead to rise. In this speech, she remembers and tries to come to terms with the tragic events of Bloody Sunday.

Carthaginians *by Frank McGuinness*

Maela

She's dead, isn't she?

Silence.

My wee girl's dead. They're running mad through the streets of Derry and my daughter's dead. Do you not understand that? (...)

Nowhere. Nowhere. I went for a walk. Through Derry. Everybody was crying. What was wrong with them? All shouting. I couldn't hear what. Was it at me? I wasn't listening to them. (...)

They said, 'She's dead. I'm afraid she's dead. We can get you home safely in an ambulance. There's a lot of bother stirring in the town.' I said, 'What do you mean she's dead? There is a dead thing in there and that thing is cancer, that thing is not my daughter. My daughter's at home. I better get back to her. I don't know what I'm doing out.' The town's gone mad today, hasn't it? (...)

No, doctor, you're wrong. My daughter is alive. My daughter is not that thing. I'm going home. (...)

Nonsense. I'm perfectly capable of walking home. At my age I should know my way around Derry. I've walked through it often enough. William Street and Shipquay Street and Ferryquay Street and the Strand and Rosville Street and Great James Street. I'm walking home through my own city. Everybody's running and everybody's crying. What's wrong? Why cry? Two dead, I hear that in William Street. I'm walking through Derry and they're saying in Shipquay Street there's five dead. I am walking to my home in my house in the street I was born in and I've forgotten where I live. I am in Ferryquay Street and I hear there's nine dead outside the Rosville flats. They opened fire and shot them dead. I'm not dead. Where are there dead in Derry? Let me look on the dead. Jesus, the dead. The innocent dead. There's thirteen dead in Derry. Where am I? What day is it? Sunday. Why is the sun bleeding? It's pouring blood. I want a priest. Give me a priest. Where am I? In Great James Street. It's full of chemists. I need a tonic for my nerves. For my head. For my heart. Pain in my heart. Breaking heart. I've lost one. I've lost them all. They had no hair. She had fire. She opened fire on herself. When I wasn't looking she caught cancer. It burned her. She was thirteen. It was Sunday. I have to go to Mass. I have to go to Mass. Dido, take me to Mass, Dido.

Patricia is the mother of two teenagers and has recently been left by her husband, Christopher. Her sister has died and her brother-in-law, Michael, has gone missing. She has left repeated messages on her estranged husband's answering machine asking for his help to find Michael. Here, she leaves yet another message. She is exhausted, confused and unaware that she is, at times, talking to herself.

Too Late For Logic *by Tom Murphy*

Patricia

Christopher. Michael. Christopher … Christopher, this is Patricia again. I'm sorry to bother you but we still can't find Michael. I've phoned and phoned. I don't know what to do. Doesn't he want to see her? Before they, before they. Doesn't he want to kiss her … I've left messages on his bloody machine, bloody machine. Bloodywell machine … doesn't he want to kiss her … Isn't there anybody there? … Come away my love my dove my fair one come away with me … My love my dove my fair one … My beloved is mine and I am his … My love my dove my … I do not understand … Michael, this is Patricia again. I've told them at the hospital that you are abroad but that you are returning. But they're getting very cross. So I've had to write the ad, the death notice for the papers. Does it suit? I don't know. That the remains will be taken to St Helen's five pm. That's tomorrow. That the burial will be on Friday at eleven. Does that suit? I hope that suits … My love, my dove my … I'm taking it in my hand or else it won't appear. And to see the undertakers again … They keep calling them caskets … And do you want a limousine? And there are papers to be signed. Always bloody papers. My beloved is mine and I am his. Certificates, affidavits, bloody papers. When someone dies, walks out, dies. I thought that if matters could not be altogether lovely ever again, they could at least be pleasant. At least that. To be signed. There are matters I am not allowed to discharge on your behalf. Enough of my own anyway. Cornelia was my sister but she was your wife. For twenty years. Does that not matter? Does that not mean something? Does anything matter? … (*A sob.*) Sorry … But I thought I had got over … (*A sob.*) Sorry … another kind of death. Thought that winter was past, the rain was over and gone. (*She starts to sob.*) Where are you my beloved. Where are you O where are you my beloved …

Ma lives in a small town on the Ulster border with her son, Donny, who is mentally disabled. In an effort to cope, she alternates beating him with a stick and smothering him with affection. In the aftermath of the killing of an RUC policeman, the house has been raided and Donny left unconscious. Here, Ma tries to revive him.

Donny Boy *by Robin Glendinning*

Ma

You'll be as right as rain son. I'll make you better just as I used to when you were still a cub. Remember how you used to come running to me with both your knees bleeding. Sure you were always a clumsy child, always tripping, falling and I was always washing the grit out of your poor knees. (*Returning with basin and a cloth.*) Now let's see … let's see … It's a wonder there's any street left the way your knees have it pummelled, the council will be after you , take an action against your Ma … (*At his side.*) Oh God Donny, that looks awful, that looks sore son, oh you poor poor lamb, you … God, it's a terrible thing to discover that something's wrong with your child. And you were a beautiful child Donny, big wide pools of eyes and a smile just for your Ma. I took you into bed with me at night ... Your Da was away in England ... no jobs for Catholics in this town. We lay in the bed, you and I, and snuggled you to me and sniffed your own, your very own wee smell just the way a bitch nuzzles her pups, and I was so happy ... so happy, then. But the months pass. The months pass. There were kids half your age running races in the street and you were still ... And then you didn't talk ... and ones round here began to look at you in a certain way ... And I lied, lied that you talked to me in the house ... Ma-ma, Da-da, Bow-wow, the whole gamut. And one day as I was recounting a particularly elevated conversation we had had about how the naughty bow wow had chased the pretty pussy up the tree I caught this one looking at me as if to say, 'You're trying hard Mrs but you're fooling no-one, God help you!' Oh a right bitch with five brats running round reciting poetry before they went to school. 'He must be very shy,' says she, 'isn't it strange a big boy of that age being so backward.' And with that her six year old comes round the corner reciting extracts from Padraig Pearse's panegyric at the graveside of O'Donavan Rossa. (*Childish voice.*) 'Oh the fools, the fools, the fools they have left us our Fenian dead.' I took you inside the hurt of it burning my face and said, 'Speak to me Donny. Say Ma, Ma, Ma, Ma, Ma, Ma, Ma, Ma, Ma, Ma! And you were silent ... silent to spite me. Say Ma! And a big tear welled up in your eye but that only angered me. 'What's the good of crying!' I raged. And I took you by your wee shoulders ... (*Doing so.*) ... and shook you and shook you and shook you and shook you ... And your head wagged back and forth like a cloth dolly ... (*It does.*) ... and I shouted and shouted, say Ma, say Ma, Ma, Ma, Ma, Ma, Ma, Ma, say Ma you stupid fucking cretin! (*She bursts into tears and buries her face in his shoulders, weeping with great heaving sobs.*) Oh God forgive me God forgive me, God ... for ... give ... me ...

Big Maggie Polpin is a middle-aged widow with a shop and farm in the South-West of Ireland. When her drunken and unfaithful husband dies, she is determined to create what she considers to be a better life for herself and her family. However, her manipulative and domineering attitude towards her children drives them away, one by one. In this speech, she tells the audience of how she was before time and disappointment hardened her.

Big Maggie *by John B. Keane*

Maggie

You know the first time, indeed the only time, I saw a penis, before I was married, was on a young garsún and he bathing in the river. It was a harmless little tassle of a thing and sure me, poor innocent me, didn't I think that they were all like that till the first night of our honeymoon. You'd think my love-life already trimmed and stunted to the marrow would have to endure no more but the awful truth was that my sex-life, my morals, my thought, word and deed were dominated by a musty old man with a black suit and a roman collar and a smell of snuff. I was suffocated by the presence of that old man. He sat in his confession-box, withering and me not knowing which way to turn for guidance. Do you know my husband never saw me naked? He never saw me white and shiny and shivering without one blemish on me from head to heel. I must have seemed as frigid and cold to him as a frozen lake. How could I thaw with my upbringing and my faith, my holy, holy faith. Maybe that's what drove him into the arms of Moll Sonders and God knows how many others. My body might say one thing but my faith always said another and my instincts were no match for that faith.

Oh I curse the stifling, smothering breath of the religion that withered my loving and my living and my womanhood. I should have been springing like a shoot of corn. I should have been singing with love, tingling, but my love never grew. 'Tis a wonder that I didn't surrender entirely to insanity in a country where it was a mortal sin to even think about another man. And there was another man. He was dark-eyed and quiet and he passed me a hundred times on the road and he'd say 'How ya there, Maggie?' and he'd give one of the cows he was driving a little tip with his ashplant and I'd say 'Fine thank you, Martin,' and he'd pass on. I saw him blush once but he never uttered one word of love to me in all those years and I longed for him. I craved him in my dreams and I thinking how lovely it would be to walk with him through the dewy fields. But he did blush.

And yet I never beamed at that man or set my cap for him or held his hand or winked at him or even gave him the faintest clue as to the names I called him and we cuddled together in those dreams. My curly ram, my sugar stick, my darling.

He's dead now that easy-going man and my husband is dead and all too soon I'll be dead but I can have anything I want for a while anyway. By God I can have any man in Ireland if there's a man I fancy and who fancies me. There's still time to fulfil myself. From now on I'll confess my fantasies to a lusty, lanky man with muscle, a man brimming with sap and tapsy, a man who'll be a real match for Big Maggie Polpin. The weal of the chastity cord is still around my belly and the incense is in my nostrils. I'm too long a prisoner but I'll savour what I can, while I can and let the last hour be the sorest.

Flora is an ageing woman, haunted by the memories of her teenage years during World War II and the losses she experienced then. She has spent time in a psychiatric hospital but now, being 'harmlessly insane', is back living in the graceful family home of her youth with her housekeeper and loyal companion, Nellie. Here, she remembers her beloved father.

The Desert Lullaby *by Jennifer Johnston*

Flora

I am a woman alone.

That was what mother used to say to make us feel bad.

Your father is battling in the desert and I am a woman alone. You have to help me by being very, very good.

She used to say it to visitors also.

Paul is battling in the desert. Then she would give a little laugh. Paul, Father, Daddy.

It was such a brave little laugh; and then someone would take her hand or touch her lightly on the shoulder, or just give a little sigh. It was his second war.

I used to feel quite sorry for him, when I thought of that.

He got the tail-end of the first one. Eighteen, straight from school.

There are pictures of him all round the house, looking so handsome in his uniform.

So ...

He was my dear friend.

He never explained to me though why he felt he had to go and leave us all. Leave poor mother to be a woman alone.

I missed him so much when he went away.

I missed him so much when he never came back.

He had this wonderful hearty laugh. He used to throw his head right back and roar with laughter. Eddie used to do that too. He had that same laugh.

At night, I used to lie in bed and7 listen and, from time to time, that laugh of his would come running to me all the way up the stairs.

He would lift me in his arms and put his lips to the side of my neck and blow warm air into my skin. I remember shivering with joy when he did that.

You'll ruin that child, Paul, mother would say.

I dreamed that I would marry him when I grew up; all in white like she had been. White lace dipping to the ground at the back and shorter in the front, showing elegant white satin shoes.

Chicken, I will love you forever, he said in my dreams and blew warm air on my neck.

Bye, chicken was what he'd said when he left, we'll meet again some sunny day. Then he threw back his head and laughed. He never even mentioned the possibility of death.

I was not in any way prepared for that.

El Alamein.

We had this map of North Africa on a table in the drawing room, with all those names on it: Tobruk, Mersa Matruh, Hemiemat, Benghazi, El Alamein.

After we got the news, she drew a little black cross by El Alamein in indelible pencil, because she wasn't able at that moment to find her pen. A few days later, she rolled up the map and put it away as if the war didn't exist any more.

We don't need any more of that was what she said.

We learnt about Khartoum at school; about General Gordon and all that sort of thing. I put up my hand and asked if Khartoum was anywhere near El Alamein.

No, said Miss Ross, Africa is rather a large place you know, Flora, and everyone giggled.

I would like to have told them about him, about the black cross in indelible pencil, but the words stuck in my mouth. Dry words, like biscuit crumbs, stuck to the roof of my mouth.

Maybe it's just as well. Sometimes there are things you should just keep to yourself.

30 MONOLOGUES FOR MEN

Dominic is a simple-minded boy who has run away from a 'special school' to which he was sent by his Uncle. He returns to the chapel in Wexford town where he had been an altar boy. The sacristan, Artie, has brought him up to the belfry to wait for someone from the school to bring him back there. Shortly after this, Dominic is killed in a car accident. Artie asks Dominic if he misses his uncle and aunt with whom he used to live.

Belfry *by Billy Roche*

Dominic

Yeah. I miss them alright Artie. And will I tell yeh what else I miss? Do yeh want to know? Chips! They'd hardly ever give yeh chips boy. I swear. Yeh think yeh were askin' for the moon or somethin' … Oh by the way Artie I have somethin' for you too … (*He takes out a key.*) Do yeh know what this is Artie. The spare key to the belfry. Little Kevin Bennett and the Dumper McGrath were ragin' when you gave this to me yeh know. 'Go away,' says the Dumper to me one day, 'with your rusty auld key to nowhere.' But what he didn't know Artie was that this is the key to the Catacombs too. I bet yeh you didn't even know that Artie did yeh? I brought the two of them down there one time and I locked them in. 'Who has a rusty auld key to nowhere now,' says I to them. The pair of them were afraid of their shit in the dark boy! … I used to take this with me everywhere I went yeh know Artie. I'd change it out of one pocket and into another whenever I'd be goin' anywhere. And do yeh want to know why Artie? Because no matter where I was – at the pictures or down in Bryne's Cafe or maybe over in the auld handball alley or somewhere – I always knew that I was the only one there who had a key to the belfry. The only one Artie! And then when I'd be goin' home in the dark after I'd take it out and I'd scrape it against the wall and I'd run along with it until the sparks came flyin' out behind me. And do yeh want to know what it was like, Artie? It was like being in the bumpers in the carnival, that's what it was like boy. The time I saw me Aunty and me Uncle goin' in the bumpers and I got a bit of a fright when I saw all the sparks comin' out of the ceilin'. I started shoutin' at them and everythin'. 'The sky's on fire,' says I but sure nobody could hardly hear me over all the noise and all. I thought the sky was on fire. (*He chuckles.*) They never even invited me to the weddin' nor nothin' boy! … You'd want to hang on to this now Artie because if anything ever happens to your key you'll need this one to get in here won't yeh? Hah? (*Artie takes the key from him.*) Spwead some jam on my bwead said Fwed I'll tell yeh one thing Artie, you're alright! …

Belfry *is the third play in* The Wexford Trilogy.

Billy is seventeen and living on the island of Inishmaan, off the west coast of Ireland, in 1934. He has been brought up by two eccentric old ladies who took him in when he was a baby, after his parents drowned. He is crippled in one arm and one leg, giving him his nickname, Cripple Billy. When a Hollywood director comes to a neighbouring island to film *Man of Aran*, Billy is desperate to escape his life of monotony by joining them. Billy persuades Babbybobby to bring him in his boat by pretending that he has only three months left to live. Billy is whisked off to America for a screen test. Four months have passed with no word from him and the islanders presume him dead by now. When he returns, he feels he owes Babbybobby – in particular – an explanation.

The Cripple of Inishmaan

by Martin McDonagh

Billy

I want to, Bobby. See, I never thought at all this day would come when I'd have to explain. I'd hoped I'd disappear forever to America. And I would've too, if they'd wanted me there. If they'd wanted me for the filming. But they didn't want me. A blond lad from Fort Lauderdale they hired instead of me. He wasn't crippled at all, but the Yank said 'Ah, better to get a normal fella who can act crippled than a crippled fella who can't fecking act at all.' Except he said it ruder. (*Pause.*) I thought I'd done alright for myself with me acting. Hours I practised in me hotel there. And all for nothing. (*Pause.*) I gave it a go anyways. I had to give it a go. I had to get away from this place, Babbybobby, be any means, just like me mammy and daddy had to get away from this place. (*Pause.*) Going drowning meself I'd often think of when I was here, just to … just to end the laughing at me, and the sniping at me, and the life of nothing but shuffling to the doctor's and shuffling back from the doctor's and pawing over the same oul books and finding any other way to piss another day away. Another day of sniggering, or the patting me on the head like a broken-brained gosawer. The village orphan. The village cripple, and nothing more. Well, there are plenty round here just as cripppled as me, only it isn't on the outside it shows. (*Pause.*) But the thing is, you're not one of them, Babbybobby, nor never were. You've a kind heart on you. I suppose that's why it was so easy to cod you with the TB letter, but that's why I was so sorry for codding you at the time and why I'm just as sorry now. Especially for codding you with the same thing your Mrs passed from. Just I thought that would be more effective. But, in the long run, I thought, or I hoped, that if you had a choice between you being codded a while and me doing away with meself, once your anger had died down anyways, you'd choose you being codded every time. Was I wrong, Babbybobby? Was I?

Joe is seventeen and lives in a small Dublin seaside town that only comes alive during the summer. He is still at school and sometimes works with his father and brother in the family chip shop. He is innocent, naive and easily impressed by his new friend, Damien, whom he is desperate to impress.

This Lime Tree Bower *by Conor McPherson*

Joe

Sunday started off normal enough.

Carmel was away with Ray, and Dad and Frank did the dinner.

They'd sort of taken over Mam's jobs about four years before, when she got really sick.

At the time I could remember her dinners and I knew that the new ones were different.

But now I couldn't remember.

I couldn't go to see her much.

I just couldn't.

One time she didn't know who I was and she got a fright when Dad told her.

She was roaring crying.

It was sick. I couldn't stand it.

I was glad when she died.

I had gotten used to her not being at home.

I didn't want to waste time getting upset. It wasn't my fault.

I didn't talk about her and I didn't like thinking about her. It scared me.

And that was all there was to it.

So anyway, after dinner on Sunday I was watching a brutal film and I was going to go up to my room, when the phone rang.

It was Damien.

There was a tickle in my stomach.

He wanted to know if I was going to Shadows.

It was a disco out near the dual carriageway.

Behind the Ancient Mariner bar.

I'd never been there and I knew my dad wouldn't let me go.

The Mariner was called the 'Bucket of Blood' because of all the fights and a barman had lost a finger once, trying to kick someone out.

Dad said it was full of gobshites and knackers.

Frank said that Shadows was crap and that the bouncers spent the whole night kicking people out, because they didn't refuse anyone. To get their money.

The bouncers would have to kick in the cubicle doors in the jacks and pull couples out who were having a quick shag.

But Frank hadn't gone there in years.

I told Damien I'd go if he was, but I had no I.D. and you had to be eighteen because there was a bar.

Damien said they never looked for I.D. if you looked anywhere near sixteen or so.

He asked me if I wanted him to get me some cans because he was going to the off licence. It was a good idea to get pissed before you went in, because the pints were £2.50.

I told him I wanted cans. But I didn't know how many to get. I didn't know how many made you drunk.

I thought I'd aim high and told him to get me ten. He laughed and told me to stop messing. But I didn't know if he meant I should ask for more or less, so I asked how many he was getting.

He said four or five. I said to get me the same.

But then he said, 'What do you want?' And I said, 'Four.' And he said, 'Four what?' And I said, 'Four cans.' 'Of what?' he said.

I said Carlsberg. Advertising works.

Jimmy Brady is good looking, charming and in his late teens. He is the local rebel in a small, southern-Irish town. He has frequently been in trouble with the police and has recently been sentenced for breaking and entering. One night, he breaks in through a broken window to the scruffy pool hall where he spends a lot of his time. He is with his girlfriend, Linda, who works in a local factory. Linda expresses sympathy for Jimmy's mother who has had to deal both with him and his abusive father. This is Jimmy's response, during which Linda draws closer to him.

A Handful of Stars *by Billy Roche*

Jimmy

I once caught them kissin' yeh know. Me Ma and Da I mean. I was only a little lad at the time. I ran out to tell Richard and when we got back me Da was singin' at the top of his voice and the two of them were waltzin' around the little kitchen. Me and Richard just stood starin' up at them. 'There they are now,' says me Da. 'James the Less and his brother Jude.' He had his good suit on him and a gleamin' white shirt and the smell of

Brylcreem off him would nearly knock you down. Me Ma was breakin' her heart laughin' at the face of us, her own face lit up like a Christmas tree. I'm not coddin' you she looked absolutely … radiant. (*Pause.*) Richard says he doesn't remember that happenin' at all. Me Ma don't either. Maybe it was just a whatdoyoucallit … a mirage.

Richard kicked me Da out of the house yeh know when I was away with the F.C.A. that time. (...)

Yeah I used to be. They threw me out of it. I got fed up of your man shoutin' at me. Whatshisname … yeh know your man lives up by you there … Brown! I told him to go and cop on himself. Anyway when I got home I found me Da stayin' down in that auld hostel. I felt terrible. He was just lyin' there, readin' a war book or somethin', a couple of those army blankets tossed across his feet. I wanted to burn the place down. I told him to get his things and come on home but he wouldn't. Well let's face it fellas like meself and me Da don't have a ghost of a chance do we? Like when I went looking for a job at your place. What did your man O'Brien ask me? What Brady are you then? Well that was me finished before I even started wasn't it?

The Howie Lee is a young Dublin man who hangs around with Ollie and Peaches – both of whom suffered severe pain and embarrassment after sleeping on a scabies-infected mattress. They are now after the Rookie Lee who was the last person to sleep on the mattress. The Howie Lee refuses to babysit his five-year-old brother, Mousey, so he can join them in their quest for revenge. The three men pursue the Rookie Lee to a bar. Ollie goes to the toilet and the Howie Lee is left sitting with Peaches and two girls they have just met.

Howie the Rookie *by Mark O'Rowe*

The Howie Lee

Dollys start talkin' among themselves. Good.
Go to say somethin' to Peaches, but he's lookin' towards the bar.
Lookin' up at The Rookie.
Not lookin', no.
Starin'.
Rememberin' the shame, his oul' fella, I can see it, the scabies' pain.
Dollys stop talkin', go quiet.
Dollys can see it too, can sense it.
Rookie at the bar.
Peaches watchin', sneerin', givin' him the evil eye.
Rookie with the fidgets, itchy, tryin' not to scratch front of the dollys.
All a-quick, Peaches can't hold it in anymore, explodes, lunges, blindsides The Rookie. I stand up. Rookie lands against the bar, Peaches lunges again, tries to sandbag him; fast an' hard, but sloppy. Rookie dodges, picks a pint off the bar, fucks it at us, dives over a table, but it's only a ha'penny dive an' he lands on top. Booze pell-mell, scrambles off, beelines for the door, he's out. But we're already runnin' across the table he dove across, then out the door, spot him, up the street, after him like The Christie; like The fuckin' Linford, flutes bouncin' around heavy an' all, sprintin' righteous, sprintin' like the Dickens, gainin'. We're gainin' good, gainin' ground, gettin' closer, movin', movin'. Down a lane he goes, best place to get him – quiet, solitary – I make a final burst, power forward, me lungs burn, me

muscles boil, I pound ahead like a thoroughbred, snortin' an' whinnyin'.
I dive.
Very smoothly. Nothin' ha'penny about *my* dive.
I'm like Tarzan.
I dive.
Like the fuckin' *Weismuller*, I am.
I dive, I sail, I take him down.
I take down my prey like a feral hunter and hold him tight as Peaches runs up, huffy and puffy, three men standin', three hearts poundin' loud, three lungs, pairs of lungs, suckin' louder, suckin' hard.
Then softer, then calmer, then quieter.
Then quiet.
Peaches lays in.
Body shots, head shots, not too hard, have to say, gently bruisin' the handsome cunt's ribs. Split lip, good one, swollen eye swellin' up. The Rookie tries to defend himself. He's feeble. I hold his arms anyway.
I hold his arms, but I'm a bit put off. Not really into it. Must be all that runnin', me stomach's queasy.
Peaches finishes off with a right-left combo to the mush, right hook to the darby.
Weak Rookie, battered Rookie drops, exhausted, Peaches breathin' hard again.
Rookie's not too hurt, drops from the run, not the hidin'.
Peaches is weak, not much weight, but he's satisfied.
We got him.
Satisfied?
Yeah.
Back to Chopper's?
Let's go.

Johnny is a young man living in London. He returns home to Dublin when his father dies. As the funeral takes place, he stays at home waiting for his family to return. Later that day, the family members reminisce and wait for guests who never turn up. In his typically provocative manner, Johnny shares a memory of his father with his family and his sister's boyfriend.

Red Roses and Petrol *by Joseph O'Connor*

Johnny

Oh really, Ma. Don't you? Well, let's tell a few stories, will we? Seeing as nobody knows any jokes. I'll start. I used to rob shops, Tom, when I was a kid. My very expensive psychiatrist has explained to me that this was all my parents' fault, because they didn't give me enough attention. But I didn't know that at the time. I thought I used to rob shops because I was a robbing pure little bastard. But there I am anyway, in Eason's, one day, and up the jumper goes this big book of poetry. Yeats's poems. Father's Day is coming up, you see, and I've no readies for a present for The Da, so. Up the ganzee goes Willie B. And I'm on my way out the door, tap on the shoulder. Up to the manager's office quick march. Why did you do it, says he. I'm disturbed, says I. The manager rings up The Da. The Da comes in firing on all cylinders, guns blazing, I mean, open for fuckin' business, Tom. He bet me from one end of Abbey Street to the other. And do you know what he did then? (...)

He took me down to the cop shop himself. (...)

Down to Store Street. And I'm crying. I mean, I'm seven. And I'm so scared that I'm pissing in my pants, Tom. And I'm begging. Please, Daddy, please, I'll never do it again. And what does The Da do? Up to the counter, knocks on it, knock, knock, knock. Big woollyback culchie guard sweating Irish stew into his armpits. What can I do for your honour? Would you ever lock this pup in a cell for the night, says The Da to the copper. I couldn't do that, sir, tis against the regulations. Out to the car, another few punches to the kidney, then home for round two. Good story isn't it? Will I go on? Do you want to hear what happened when I failed the leaving cert? Or maybe Catherine's told you.

Michael is twenty-eight and – until recently – has worked as a waiter in his native Westmeath. He has just moved into a house of flats in Dublin. He is hopeful of finding a job in hotel management and optimistic that he will fit into his chaotic new home. Tony and Christine are neighbours also living in the house. He rings his mother for the first time from the phone downstairs.

Home *by Paul Mercier*

Michael

Hello, how ye?
It's me, yeah … on the hotline. (*Chuckles*)
No, on the hot … I'm jokin', Ma, forget it … I said …
Yes, I reversed charges, ye see, because I didn't have …
Listen, I'll pay for it. Promise. I just couldn't manage it this end that's all. Who? Christine.
No, Ma, she's eh a neighbour. Yes. She just called by to say hello.

I know. I'm sorry … Like I had it in mind to ring last night but there was …

No, there isn't any, ye see. I'm ringin' from a phone box down the street … That's right.

No, I have a toilet and bathroom, okay … of my own, yes … but no phone, no. No, Ma, I told you, she's a neighbour.

Listen, how are ye, tell us? … You managing okay?

No, I don't think it's a silly question at all. I'm only asking.

Ah for cryin' out loud, I wouldn't be ringin' if I didn't care …

Ma, don't … Not this again, please.

I did not storm out. There was a train to catch.

No, not next weekend. Well, I don't know when.

For goodness sake, I've only just got here.

Enter Tony from his room. Michael laughs into the phone pretending that he's hearing a joke. Tony exits into other room.

Look, I'll ring again.

Tomorrow.

Turn off that immersion, won't you?

Lock all doors. Right. And plug out that television.

Yeah.

Bye.

It's for the better, Ma.

Bye.

Hangs up, relieved and exits out the front door.

Michael Collins – representing the historical figure – is a courageous, charismatic man committed to the fight for Irish independence. Here, he is the Minister for Finance and Director of Intelligence. Collins is attracted to a number of beautiful, fascinating women with whom he has passionate affairs. He has been arguing with Minister for Defence, Cathal Brugha, about Collins' policy of ambushing the enemy. He now addresses the audience.

Good Evening, Mr Collins *by Tom McIntyre*

Collins

We live in the hour of the body or the lash: who'll yield first? Just got word the old family place was burned down, house, outbuildings. 'Selective Reprisals', the papers call it. My brother says they'd have burned the seventy acres only they'd other houses awaiting the torch. I loved that place – everyone, no doubt, says that – but it *was* special. Everyone says that too … The barn … I think of that barn a lot … Hay, swallows, a ladder hanging on a wall – the longest ladder in the world it seemed to me, too long ever to be used, maybe it was just there – for example … Once when I was (*gesture*) that size, I was playing in the loft with the sisters … I was brought up surrounded by women – an oul wan told me once – *That'll always stand to you* … But the loft, the floor of the loft, this particular day, was covered with flowers. I can see them yet. There we are playing garden of an afternoon. There was this trapdoor at one end of the loft, and nothing would do me but to find it – even if I didn't know I was searching for it … I rambled my way to it – the foxglove looking at me, the clover smelling, the daisies basking, the buttercups shiny – and, the trapdoor somehow not fastened – I'm gone, fifteen-foot drop to the stable below. A lap of hay was all that saved me. It wasn't, they said, supposed to be there – but it was. I was asked once – What do you believe in? A lap of hay, I said. May it always be there for you, was the wish came back.

Gene Brady is a Protestant farmhand in his early thirties. He worked in Fermanagh for Hubert Murray – a Republican gunman – and had an affair with his employer's wife, Rhoda, before leaving to live in New York. When Hubert is supposed dead from an explosion, Gene returns with plans to take Rhoda back to America with him. However, Hubert has only feigned death and arranges to kill Gene. Some weeks later, Rhoda kills her husband. The ghosts of Gene and Hubert meet and relive events leading up to their deaths. Gene has been unable to remember how he died until this speech.

Hubert Murray's Widow *by Michael Harding*

Gene

I remember now. I got into the car with Enda. It was dark. Middle of the night. Me hands were tied behind me back, and Enda had me by the hair, and he was dragging me from the car. He was dragging me into the forest, and I thought, Jesus, Jesus, I thought, he's gonna shoot me, the Lord is my shepherd, there is nothing I shall want, I thought, Jesus, he's gonna do it, Enda. Like he's done before, and then go home and demolish a bottle of whiskey, there was only me and him, this is more intimate than sex I thought. I'm with this man and he is going to blow me brains out, 'Our help is in the name of the Lord', I said, out loud, 'Shut up', says he. 'A, Jesus, Enda. Don't,' says I. Pulling me hair. 'For the Lord shall be with us in the day of tribulation', I says. 'Fuck up', says he, 'ye mad bastard'. 'Can I not pray?' I said. Oh, Jesus, he won't even let me pray. And then I thought of that single dollar note, I brought it with me from New York. It was me good luck charm. I changed everything for sterling at the airport, but I kept this dollar, lucky charm, it meant I would be going back again. It was my promise to Manhattan. Me hands were tied. Enda was emptying me pockets. I was crying. I kept praying he wouldn't find the dollar note. And then I seen him hold it. And laughing. And he was saying, 'You won't be needing this anymore'. And then (...)

And then I seen you. (*Kneels.*) And I says, 'Ah, Jesus, Mr Murray, don't shoot me. No. You wouldn't shoot poor Eugene would you? I'm sorry. I'm sorry. I'm so sorry'. And I kept thinking about me lucky charm. Me dollar. I wanted to hold it. If I could just have that I wouldn't mind. A Jesus Mr Murray.

Eoin is an Irishman in his early thirties who is now living and working in Germany. Eoin, Mick and Shane have been friends since school – drawn together by their love of football. Their dedication has led them all around Europe following the Irish soccer team. It is 19 June 1988 during the European Championship and Eoin is in Altona railway station, Hamburg, just after midnight. He has discovered the previous day that he is soon to become a father. He has just been to the Ireland versus Holland match and he relives the final moments of the match as the Dutch team is winning. If Ireland loses, Eoin feels that it will mean the end – not only of the team's involvement in the Championship, but also of his youth and the three friends' journey together.

In High Germany *by Dermot Bolger*

Eoin

He raises the scarf once more in the air and screams:

Ireland! Ireland! Ireland!

He lowers the scarf, suddenly weary.

And then the final whistle blew. I lowered my head feeling suddenly old. The players sank down, knees pressed into the turf, as the Dutch celebrated. And after a few minutes when I looked around none of us were moving as the Dutch fans filed away, muted and relieved, down that avenue of stone.

He turns around to look behind him for a second.

And when they were gone we turned, solid to a man and a woman, thirteen thousand of us, cheering, applauding, chanting out the players' names, letting them know how proud we felt. I thought of my father's battered travel-light bag, of Molloy drilling us behind that 1798 pike, the wasters who came after him hammering *Peig* into us, the masked men blowing limbs off passers-by in my name. You know, all my life, it seems, somebody somewhere has always been trying to tell me what Ireland I belonged in. But I only belonged there. I raised my hands and applauded, having finally, in my last moments with Shane and Mick, found the only Ireland whose name I can sing, given to me by eleven men dressed in green. And the only Ireland I can pass on to the son who will carry my name in a foreign land.

I thought of my uncles and my aunts scattered through England and the States, of every generation culled and shipped off like beef on the hoof. And suddenly it seemed they had found a voice at last, that the Houghtons, the McCarthys, the Morrises were playing for all those generations written out of history. And I knew they were playing for my children to come too, for Shane's and Mick's, who would grow with foreign accents and Irish faces, bewildered by their fathers' lives.

All thirteen thousand of us stood on the terrace, for fifteen, twenty minutes after the last player had vanished, after Houghton had returned, forlornly waving a tricolour in salute, after Jack had come back out to stand and stare in wonder at us. Coffin ships, the decks of cattle boats, the departure lounges of airports. We were not a chosen generation, the realization of a dream, any longer. We were a hiccough, a brief stutter in the system. Thirteen thousand stood as one on that German terrace before scattering back towards Ireland and out like a river bursting its banks across a vast continent.

He steps down from the seat and puts the scarf around his neck.

I did not need to look at Shane or Mick. We knew that part of our lives was over for ever. We had always returned together once, a decade spent in a limbo of youth, poker sessions and parties in bedsits, football in Fairview Park on Sunday mornings before the pubs opened, walking out the long roads to Phibsborough and Rathmines on Saturday nights with sixpacks and dope and a sense of belonging so ingrained we were never aware of it.

He throws the pack up on his shoulder and turns, speaking in Shane's accent:

'Italy, 1990, lads,' Shane said. 'We'll be there.'

(His own voice:) But we knew we wouldn't, even if Ireland was, knew we were fractured, drifting apart. Jesus, we all felt so old suddenly.

(Shane's accent:) 'We did it,' Shane said. 'We were part of it.'

Jody is in his early thirties and has a young son who is being brought up by another man. He has returned home after an absence of some years. He is visiting the man he has always called 'father' – although he has been told that the old man is not his natural father. It is the eve of a potential nuclear war and the two men are transforming the house into a primitive fall-out shelter. The time spent together in the enclosed room forces Jody to explore his role as both a son and a father. The old man has fallen asleep, giving Jody the opportunity to look closely at him.

Long Black Coat *by John Waters*

Jody

Dad. Are you awake? *(There is no answer. Jody walks around the sleeping figure of the old man, examining him in minute detail.)*

What are you like? Where, in the name of Jesus, did they spring you from? Who are you to me? I woke up and found you there. And me? I might be a man from Mars, for all I know. It wouldn't surprise me in the least, to wake up one morning and find that me face had turned green and I'd sprouted two fucken aerials from the top of me head. There you are now, I'd say. (*He picks up more books.*) I must be about my father's business. (*He looks around the room.*) And this here. This is as plausible as anything else. (*Goes to barricaded window but, unable to see out, gestures towards street outside.*) That street out there. Home. That's a good one. In the beginning was the sound of the street. It said something … The. World. Is. Not. Your. Friend. I would lie in bed listening to the sounds at night. The cars growing nearer and nearer … Vrrrrmmmmmmmmm. Mmmmmmmmmmmmm-mmmm. Mmmmmmmmmmmmmmm … (*Mimics car noises.*) until you could make out the distinct sounds that gave them away. Every exhaust with a rattle to match the face of its driver. And then in the morning to walk through those streets to eight o'clock Mass. The scent of the new rain on the breeze-dried dust, like the taste of a penny on the tongue. The town I had been told to call home. Not only had the town been here before I was born but the thoughts that made up the lives of the people who had somehow built this street in its particular configuration, with just that colour of concrete, that narrowness of window, that shape of doorway. (*Makes sound of a football crowd roar.*) Ahhhhhhhh-hhhhhhhhhhhhhhhhhhhhhhhhhhhhhhhhhh. Ahhhhhhhhhhhh-hhhhhhhhhrrrrrrgggggggggggggggggggghhhhh. My tiny hand shelled within yours. Big and bony. Aaaaaahhhhhhhhhhhhh-hhhhhhhhhhhhhh. "He's at the forty yard line he's at the thirty-five he's at the thirty he swerves he stops he turns he kicks and its … over the bar and its a point a point another point for the Big Man from North Kerry". And you tightening your grip on my hand and sighing softly, "Themselves and their football." Nothing moved except ourselves, as though the sun had put the town to sleep with the wireless on. The smell of dinner and polish that always came from other people's homes. Father and son, for all the world might know. Me taking in this strange man, this figure inside in this long black coat. (*Pauses.*) Or arriving into the bar with its polished wood and the smell of a thousand different drinks. "How's the youngfellah?" "It's great to be young, but the young never get to know that til it's too late." "You cannot tell a young person how short life is." "True for you. True for you. These are the best days of your life, youngfellah, d'ya hear that?" I loved to listen to the way you would talk. This was the only way I ever knew you. It was in these moments I grew to like you, when I could see that others liked you, and to regard me as someone worthwhile on that account. Sometimes, still, we make sense to one another. A little. I dunno. A private joke maybe. I never laugh as truly as at one of those. But then it's gone. And: silence. Well, not silence … talk, noise … It's like we lost our language or something – the language we both understood. Even the things we talk about do not belong to us. They're not our concern, except at some superficial level of our lives. We pluck them from the air like crab apples. More often they fall between us and we say something in surprise. I watch you with your cue cards, writing down every fiddle-fart some gobshite says on … that yoke. Trying to hold on to the world. Trying to TALK TO ME! That fucken man. (*Bangs table with book.*) Jesus!

Cahill Smith has a reputation for being heavily involved in the IRA. He has been nicknamed the Quartermaster since he drove an abandoned sausage van to a barricade and fed the rioters when he was fifteen years old. Following the murder of Thompson – an RUC policeman – Cahill has forced the simple-minded Donny and his Ma to hide the murder weapon, after which their house is raided by the British army. When he returns to retrieve the gun, Ma begins to suspect that Cahill is, in fact, an informer and that he did not kill Thompson, as she had been led to believe. The anxious and desperate Cahill is eventually forced to tell the truth about his involvement with the IRA and with Thompson.

Donny Boy *by Robin Glendinning*

Cahill

I tried to join, dammit. They wouldn't have me. They said I had too high a profile. I was an eejit. A joker. Too wild. Too bloody well known for my own good or theirs. They laughed at me. 'Go bring us a van full of sausages,' they said, 'only this time don't forget the chips, ha ha ha ha ha.' 'Fuck youse', I said to myself. Mrs, I have nothing. No job, no qualifications, no hope; I can't leave me oul fella and he's been on the dole so long he can't remember what a shovel looks like. 'Go bring us a van full of sausages and chips, we could do with a good feed, ha ha ha ha ha ha.' Fuck youse. This town is rigged against me and even my own don't trust me. 'I'll show youse I'm no frigging sausage man.' And I did. And I kept quiet. I had to. Stayed out of trouble. I was determined to show them. I didn't even spend the money Thompson gave me, I hid it. Oh I kept a low profile alright. Two weeks ago I was sent for. Sent for? As sure as God I thought they'd found out and were going to shoot me. 'You've changed your ways,' they said. 'You're a new man. You've impressed us Cahill and now we've a job for you.' By Jesus I was in! I was one of the boys! 'We want you to mind a gun,' they said. 'We want you to stay out of trouble, to keep a low profile,' they said. 'We'll send you word.' I forgot all about Thompson then. I just put it behind me. As if it hadn't happened. The word came and I did what I was told. I was as proud as proud as I slipped along the shadowy side of the street, the gun in my pocket and fuck, there was Thompson winding down the window of his car. 'Is that you Cahill?' he said.

'Yeh', I said.

'It's time we had a wee word Cahill,' he said.

'Is it?' I said, and watched him step out of the car.

'Cahill, oul son, you and I are at the proverbial crossroads,' he said.

'Is that so, Mr Thompson?' I said, but I was thinking the same thing myself.

'Up to now Cahill, me oul segocia, we've been dealing in peanuts. Now, Cahill this game is far too bloody serious for peanuts. We don't want to be risking our lives for a load of gravel shit, do we? You know what I mean Cahill?'

'Yeh', I said.

'Well, have you got anything for me, Cahill? Anything worthwhile that is, anything worth risking a pair of lives?'

'Yeh', I said. 'Yeh, Mr Thompson, I have.'

'Good boy,' he said. 'Let's have it and I'll make it really worth your while.'

He was lighting a cigarette and I stepped up to him and said, 'Here it is, Mr Thompson, Sir.'

'Now where did you get that, Cahill?' he said. I plugged him three times. (*Pause.*) He pleaded … 'please' … I plugged him again … And there was still a wee pulse throbbing in his neck and … and … (*Breaking down.*) I said an act of contrition and ran.

Kenneth Pyper is an Ulster man in his thirties who has enlisted in the British Army during World War I. He is the eldest son – and black sheep – of a wealthy Protestant family. After five months in the trenches, he is back in Ulster on leave. He is on Boa Island, Lough Erne, with David Craig who has saved Pyper's life on the battlefield. Here, he tells Craig – with whom he is in love – about an incident from his past when he lived in France.

Observe the Sons of Ulster Marching Towards the Somme *by Frank McGuinness*

Pyper

She killed herself. She killed herself. She killed herself. Because she was stupid enough to believe that I was all she had to live for. Me. What would I have brought her? The same end, but a lot later, and not with the dignity of doing it with her own hand. I'm one of the gods, I bring destruction. Remember? (...)

What's more to be said? She took her life. She did something with it, finally and forever. I thought I was doing the same when I cleared out of this country and went to do something with my heart and my eyes and my hands and my brains. Something I could not do here as the eldest son of a respectable family whose greatest boast is that in their house Sir Edward Carson, saviour of their tribe, danced in the finest gathering Armagh had ever seen. I escaped Carson's dance. While you were running with your precious motors to bring in his guns, I escaped Carson's dance, David. I got out to create, not destroy. But the gods wouldn't allow that. I could not create. That's the real horror of what I found in Paris, not the corpse of a dead whore. I couldn't look at my life's work, for when I saw my hands working they were not mine but the hands of my ancestors, interfering, and I could not be rid of that interference. I could not create. I could only preserve. Preserve my flesh and blood, what I'd seen, what I'd learned. It wasn't enough. I was contaminated. I smashed my sculpture and I rejected any woman who would continue my breed. I destroyed one to make that certain. And I would destroy my own life. I would take up arms at the call of my Protestant fathers. I would kill in their name and I would die in their name. To win their respect would be my sole act of revenge, revenge for the bad joke they had played on me in making me sufficiently different to believe I was unique, when my true uniqueness lay only in how alike them I really was. And then the unseen obstacle in my fate. I met you.

John Joe Moran lives in the claustrophobic atmosphere of a small town in the rural Ireland of 1958. He is thirty-three years old, lives with his parents and earns a meagre wage as a grocer's assistant. He has to borrow money from his mother in order to go out with his girlfriend, Mona, who is in her early twenties and works in the bank. At this point in the play, John Joe is anxious to emigrate – taking Mona with him and leaving behind the small-minded gossip and begrudgery of his home town. His brother, Frank, is already in America (although he has been in jail there) but his friend, Pakey Garvey, is doing very well in England. John Joe has particularly vivid dreams. Here, we see him sitting up in bed, delighted in this fantasy of his new address.

A Crucial Week in the Life of a Grocer's Assistant *by Tom Murphy*

John Joe

And how are you now, John Joe? Very well thank you. And how do you like England? Very well thank you. But it's America. Very well thank you. Your address? – What? Your address – Oh! Your address – Yes. Two-two-two A, Tottenham Court Road, Madison Square Gardens, Lower Edgebaston, Upper Fifth Avenue, Camden Town, U.S.A., S.W.6. And it's very nice over here. I made it! – I made it! No pot lately shined calls the kettle black. Everyone's pink like the image of God. My room – My address – Well, look at it – look at it! The walls, white walls, not cluttered, but Spring; no trespassers jarring the trembling. Look at those fields, the first soft grass! Look at the bracken, the smell of the bog, and Gardenfield Wood whispering to Molloy! I made it! – I got here! Sure Pakey Garvey isn't free at all. Or Frank, poor Frank. But there's no flies on me. And no bitterness, mind. And they're all right at home. No, they didn't have to die! She told me she smelt the primroses once, a print dress and her hair, walking Cloonasscragh. God bless you, I said. Say it again. God bless them, I say, and was free with a smile, obviously right for emigration. I got here, I got here! See that box over there? Treasure, gold. Big box – the big box – bigger box – the biggest one! To be sent home to Mammy, cause now I'm of use. And, oh, there's nothing futile about you, John Joe. No-no, but sensible, practical, reasonable, logical. And I shall have some peace here. Breathe in. (*He starts to inhale. There's a knock at the door. He gasps, alarmed.*) Ah! (*But almost immediately his delight returns.*) Aaaa! That will be Monda, Mona, Mo-o-na, making a nice, clean, civilized and useful visit. (*Second knock at the door; he smiles.*) I always let my wife knock three times to prove the point of my privacy. I'm very happy now.

Lenny is a thirty-three year old trombone player living in Belfast in 1974. He and his wife, Marion, had a five month old baby who died five years ago. Since then, Lenny and Marion have been separated and are in the process of getting a divorce. An all-out loyalist strike has thrown the couple together again as they have been practically under siege in a house inherited recently by Lenny. Also in the house are an abused wife of an RUC officer and a friend of Lenny's who is home from Birmingham. The political situation is resolving itself somewhat for the time being and, during the early hours of Pentecost Sunday, Lenny returns to the house after playing a gig. He tunes a banjo as stories and memories are exchanged.

Pentecost *by Stewart Parker*

Lenny

There was something happened to me last summer – as it happens – last August, down near Kinsale. (*He sets the banjo aside*) There's a Dutch guy with a pub there, runs a lot of jazz nights. This particular night went on till half-six in the morning, the sun was hanging out, I was ready for a look at the ocean, so was the lady vocalist. She was a strange woman, half gipsy, from Sligo or somewhere weird like that, totally wrecked on everything on offer, which was plenty … so. We stumbled down to this cove, a lovely horseshoe of sand, except her and me couldn't handle any more bright lights, so we collapsed on to a sheltered bit of grass behind some boulders. And your woman starts crooning. (*Sings*) "Just a closer walk with thee …" lying there splayed out in the warm singing away … and she begins to peel her clothes off. Nothing to do with me – she was stretched out flat with her eyes closed – but before too long, she's entirely bare, the voice floating in the early breeze. (*Sings*) "Grant it Jesus if you please …" and I'm hunkered down beside her, with a swollen mouth from playing all night, staring out at the glittery water, stunned all over, the way you are. And then, into my line of vision – there comes this sight, at first I thought I was hallucinating, it was a gaggle of nuns, real nuns, in the whole gear, which they were busy stripping off, over their heads. There was a dozen or more of them. It was a nuns' swimming party. Underneath their habits, they had these interlock jobs, sort of vests and baggy long johns. I suppose they reckoned at that hour there'd be nobody to see them. So down they pelted into the sea, frisking around and frolicking like nine-year-olds, the noise of it – while your woman is meanwhile stretched out starkers beside me, singing this deep-throated heartfelt version of "Just a Closer Walk With Thee" … entirely oblivious … and the nuns are splashing each other, and giggling and screaming, and flinging themselves about in the golden light, with the wet interlock clinging to their excited bodies – and it doesn't take a lot to see that the nuns are experiencing their sex and the vocalist her spirit. And for a crazy few seconds I all but sprinted down to the nuns to churn my body into theirs, in the surf foam, and then bring them all back to the lady vocalist, for a session of great spirituals … and maybe that's how it was … what it was like here. Before Christianity. Is what I'm saying.

Kenneth Norman McCallister is a thirty-four year old Protestant man, married with young children and living in Belfast. He works as a clerk in a social welfare office. His background is a loyalist one and he has inherited a legacy of bigotry and hatred which he has never questioned. Kenneth has just been accepted as a member of a prestigious golf club – a status which has been denied to his Catholic boss, Jerry. Here, he remembers a day when Jerry is having trouble with his car. Kenneth gives him a lift home, driving through a Catholic part of the city for the first time. He goes into Jerry's house for a drink.

A Night in November *by Marie Jones*

Kenneth

I had pictured Jerry's house in my head, well, it couldn't be up to much I'd thought … he did live in West Belfast and we grew up with the pictures of deprivation and filth and graffiti and too many kids and not enough soap … well, there it was, bigger than mine … detached with a garage, the lawn strewn with bikes and scooters and toy tractors, strewn with life, not like ours, manicured to the last blade … the unwritten rule BIKES AND SCOOTERS FORBIDDEN EXCEPT ON THE CONCRETE PROVIDED … grey cold concrete especially laid so the kids wouldn't ruin the grass … the grass was for show, concrete could be scrubbed afterwards … and inside Jerry's house was a whole other life, a life I've never known, a life of disorder … books upside down in the bookcase, not in order of size or colour … in our house only properly bound ones went on show … Debrah's order from the book club … burgundy leather bound classics … never opened, but they suit the bookshelf, match the wallpaper, blend in with the carpet, books that can't be allowed to vary just like the fitted kitchens. I once wanted to order a couple of Stephen King's from the book club, unbound … No, Kenneth, we are not spending all that money on something that has to be hidden away in a drawer and I accepted it, of course I accepted it, God help me … and there in Jerry's house, books of all shapes and sizes, books that looked read, had dog ears, piles and piles of them and I was jealous of Jerry and his disordered life and his higgledy-piggledy books.

'Fraid I can't offer you anything to eat, Kenny, I have to cook m'own the night, and I don't think that you would want to wait around while I burn it.

Wife not here, Jerry.

No, she's left a note on the kitchen table, she took a notion to take the kids to the pictures, so I'm to get my own.

Oh, God, what freedom, what wonderful unpredictability … and then at the bottom of the note which I strained my eyes to see, what Jerry never bothered to read out … Love You … why should he bother to read that out, it's a fact, it's unspoken, it's taken as read, but she still writes it, as a matter of course, just to make sure Jerry knows, but Jerry does know, so it doesn't matter if Jerry ever gets into the Golf Club because Jerry is loved by his wife, who still tells him … you lucky bastard, where did it all go wrong for me … where … how … why.

I drank the beer and left … I didn't want to go home, to be there when Debrah came in from aerobics … the woman I fell in love with had vanished into the perfect ten-by-ten square of our designed life, bound to the burgundy unopened classics and the scrubbed concrete … and me, her husband, the man she fell in love with tied to order and loyalty and nothing.

Bat is a 1916 Citizen Army veteran and works as a pawnshop assistant. When his son, Rabbit, grows up, he works his way up from nothing to become a haulage magnate. As this one-man show progresses, Rabbit becomes so obsessed with the memory of his father, that his mind and body are sometimes taken over by Bat, as is the case in this instance. Here, Bat is chastising Rabbit for breaking his mother's heart and remembering the day Mamie and himself got a new enamel bath.

Bat the Father, Rabbit the Son

by Donal O'Kelly

Bat

Ah you make me sad to think I – I … well, Mamie, you know, bore you. Where was I? And the bath had a good ten eleven inches and the water still hot, and the steam made the kitchen hot we were both in our pelt – goosepimples, yeah, but not from the weather – and no jokey-joking now, dance a little slower, my hands were lifting up your breasts just a little, oh Mamie what a lovely – weight, and you with your hands front and back and up and down and rubbing me all over and your lips on the side of my necky-neck 'cause you didn't like the blood around my lip – understandable enough – and your hands were back and front and up and down and back and up again and then, then you dipped your toe in –

– Just another bit of cold, I think, you said and then – And sure then we started giggling again watching the ripples and splashing our hands and then we tumbled in thank God (*Down in behind the side of the bath.*) taking care not to bump your head on the big brass taps.

– Oh Jesus it's great, you said, and squeezed me to you.

– Are you all right, I said.

– Am I all right you *amadán*!? Do you think I'm sick or what!? And you rubbed the Sunlight soap on my shoulders that you always called my ballcocks.

– Are you sure, says I.

– Oh yes, says you.

– I hope you don't drown, says I, only joking half.

– Oh it's lovely, says you, sure what a way to go don't you think in our new enamel bath.

– Oh-ho Mamie my love and so smooth, smooth, smooth oh buttery, but Mamie, the water might go in ahead and harm, you know, the insides –

– Ah blather me shite, do you think it's a bloody bung-hole down there lovey lovey dovey God above that's the way my darling revolutionary –

Sure then I didn't care a damn, thrashing in the water lovely feeling mind you – and the four pigs' trotters underneath holding up the bath no bother, and we both came together like a fairy tale finish with a roar and then a shshshsh 'cause the people next door and a rake of plates came sliding off the draining-board and landed on the backs of my legs … But none of them broke! Thanks be to Jaysus! Oh Mamie, Mamie …

John Foster is from Northern Ireland and is the product of a complex, mixed religious background. He was an agent for British Army Intelligence but had his job taken from him and now works in supermarket security. He returns home from England for his mother's funeral. In this one-man play, he goes to the attic and wears old clothes, becoming various members of his family, as he prepares to commit suicide. He puts on one of his mother's dresses and – during this speech – he takes on her persona.

Hard to Believe *by Conall Morrison*

Foster

When my mother was three years old her mother caught TB. They were pretty poor, she was pretty weak, she knew she wasn't going to live long; so she set to and made clothes for her daughter for when she would be aged four, and five, and six, up until eleven, mapping out the young life she knew she wasn't going to see. And after his wife's death, my grandfather filed all the clothes away in a chest of drawers and told my mother not to be poking and prying, they'd come when they'd come. But sometimes, when he was out working on the farm, she'd sneak upstairs, open the drawers and dress up in the clothes of the years to come, imagining what was ahead, what her mother foresaw for her.

When she reached twelve and had outgrown the last contents of the top drawer, she refused the offer of new clothes from her father and squeezed into the old ones until she burst out of them and they fell apart. And then she kept all the scraps in a bundle in the attic, until moths and mildew destroyed the lot.

Cup and saucer.

Oh, it helped me to remember John, it helped me to remember … the threads of my life! Yes. Oh, I remember … the watery soup the year round and the Christmas goose killed with the razor blade; and the children in limbo, up a rung with every prayer; and the banshee screaming in the ditch because the devil was mad if a soul got into heaven; oh, the cattle markets and my father robbed blind every year; the lovely tassels on the priest's garments.

Stop your noise.

And the dead cardinals' hats hanging by threads in Armagh Cathedral; and lighting candles to saints and the flames flickering up like prayers; and the two cathedrals on the facing hills like the twin horns of a dilemma; oh, the stained glass windows with colours that were a wee glimpse of heaven; and the money for masses for the living, the dead and the haunted.

Stop footering with that.

The Far East and the nuns with men's names; and hand-me-downs from England; and conniptions because of the priest calling; and the black spot on my tongue that the Devil put there for my lies; and my gleaming white dress for my first communion; and very little money that Sunday because I had few relatives; and the tea, the cups of tea. Here you, get that kettle on, careful now.

Casimir is in his thirties and is the only son of the authoritarian District Justice O'Donnell. He was educated at boarding school, abandoned his law studies and now works part-time in a food processing factory in Hamburg where he lives with his wife, Helga, and their three sons. In the mid-1970s – after an absence of eleven years – he has returned to the decaying Ballybeg Hall for his sister's wedding. He is shy, uneasy and his exaggerated mannerisms give an impression of eccentricity. During his visit, his father dies and the day of the wedding is replaced by a funeral. He gets confused about events from the past, often romanticising his memories. Here, Casimir is talking to his brother-in-law, Eamon, about growing up in Ballybeg Hall.

Aristocrats *by Brian Friel*

Casimir

I discovered a great truth when I was nine. No, not a great truth; but I made a great discovery when I was nine – not even a great discovery but an important, a very important discovery for me. I suddenly realized I was different from other boys. When I say I was different I don't mean – you know – good Lord, I don't for a second mean I was – you know – as they say nowadays 'homosexual' – good heavens I must admit, if anything, Eamon, if anything I'm – (*Looks around.*) – I'm vigorously hetero-sexual ha-ha. But of course I don't mean that either. No, no. But anyway. What I discovered was that for some reason people found me … peculiar. Of course I sensed it first from the boys at boarding-school. But it was Father with his usual – his usual directness and honesty who made me face it. I remember the day he said to me: 'Had you been born down there' – we were in the library and he pointed down to Ballybeg – 'Had you been born down there, you'd have become the village idiot. Fortunately for you, you were born here and we can absorb you.' Ha-ha. So at nine years of age I knew certain things: that certain kinds of people laughed at me; that the easy relationships that other men enjoy would always elude me; that – that – that I would never succeed in life, whatever – you know – whatever 'succeed' means – (...)

No, no, please. That was a very important and a very difficult discovery for me, as you can imagine. But it brought certain recognitions, certain compensatory recognitions. Because once I recognized – once I acknowledged that the larger areas were not accessible to me, I discovered – I had to discover smaller, much smaller areas that were. Yes, indeed. And I discovered that if I conduct myself with some circumspection, I find that I can live within these smaller, perhaps very confined territories without exposure to too much hurt. Indeed I find that I can experience some happiness and perhaps give a measure of happiness, too. My great discovery. Isn't it so beautiful? (*Music.*) Somehow the hall doesn't exist without him.

Patrick Kirwan is a gentle, awkward, forty-year-old lithographer from Cork City. He now lives and works in Baltimore, County Cork. In the 1890s, he meets and falls in love with Fanny Hawke, a thirty-year-old member of a dwindling, Quaker-like sect, originally from Manchester but now living on Sherkin Island. The Hawkes pray for God to send a husband from Manchester for Fanny. In marrying Patrick, she would have to leave her religion and her family behind on Sherkin. Patrick travels across to the island – and stays in its uncomfortable hotel – in the hope of meeting Fanny. It is early in the morning. Patrick is in bed in his bare room – he has not slept.

Prayers of Sherkin *by Sebastian Barry*

Patrick

There are fish in the mortar of this wall and they are not fossils. It is that damp, they're swimming around in it. I have been in Glasgow, where they have many cheap hotels for cheap travellers. Pity, pity to the man who must spend his life in such a room as this. (*Rubbing his face, scratching his thigh.*) I thought I'd had my allotment of fleabites in this life. I was brother to many generations of fleas in my youth. Well, that's how we lived. There isn't any need for nobility. I will never keep a cat. That's the most vicious fleas. I think Fanny Hawke has a clear head. I think she is much the best, much the best. Still, I never saw one like her, so I don't know. Maybe she's a ghost. A sort of vision, in her terms. I think maybe Baltimore is a vision too. A hellish one. Of course it is myself that is the vision. Of misery. The fleas are taking great nourishment from a vision none the less. Christ, (*Trapping a flea.*) that's not a flea, that's the whole dog. Maybe it is wrong of me to take a visionary child away from her island, or seek to. But I can do no other thing. If I require to be forgiven, forgive me. I'm following only before a thing that's far wickeder and blinder than myself. Not so wicked, no, not so wicked. In this fashion I would say, I love her. Was there ever love more foolish or more forceful? I have a fire under my arse, and it isn't only made by the mouths of fleas. My head even is just a hearth. You could leave spuds in it at night and take them to school in the morning, in the frost. Christ, I am lost for this bright woman. I have to submit. (*Strikes palm on bed like a wrestler.*) I submit. Take that twist off my arm. And I will not be put away from her. I'll be greater than I am. I'll be subtle, I'll be a real dancer. No one will know me. I'll get a shock in mirrors. Ah, I'll weep wicked tears if she'll even hear me. I swear it. I'll lose my legs as well as my heart. She'll slay me. And I'll rejoice. I'll send penny cards to all my acquaintance, saying, Fanny Hawke killed me. That is the better sort of murder. And may God give me good words for her, give me words.

Francis Hardy is an Irish, middle-aged faith healer who has tried to make a living by performing one-night stands in the villages of Scotland and Wales. He travelled with his wife, Grace, and manager, Teddy, experiencing a few small triumphs, many disappointments and some personal tragedies en route. When Frank felt his talent was abandoning him, he returned home to Ireland for the first time in years. He arrived at a lounge bar in the village of Ballybeg, near Donegal Town, with Grace and Teddy. Here, Frank describes his version of what happened there when he agreed to cure a young crippled man. Frank knows with absolute certainty that he would not succeed and that he would be brutally murdered as a result.

Faith Healer *by Brian Friel*

Frank

When we came downstairs to the lounge in the pub we got caught up in the remnants of a wedding party – four young men, locals, small farmers, whose friend had just gone off on his honeymoon a few hours earlier. Good suits. White carnations. Dark, angular faces. Thick fingers and black nails. For a while they pretended to ignore us. Then Ned, the biggest of them, asked bluntly who we were and what we were. Teddy told them. 'Dear 'eart ... the ... most ... sensational ... fantastic.' And either at the extravagance of the introduction or because of an unease they suddenly exploded with laughter and we were embraced. We formed a big circle and drank and chatted. Gracie sang – 'Ilkley Moor'? – something like that. Teddy entertained them with tales of our tours ranging from the outrageous to the maudlin and ended with his brown eyes moist with tears: 'Dear 'earts, the insights it 'as given me into tortured 'umanity.' And I told myself that I was indeed experiencing a home-coming. All irony was suspended.

Then suddenly a man called Donal who had scarcely spoken up to this thrust a bent finger in front of my face and challenged, 'Straighten that, Mr Hardy.' And the bar went still.

I caught the finger between the palms of my hands and held it there and looked into his face. Already he was uneasy – he wanted to withdraw the challenge. He began to stammer how the accident happened – something about a tractor, a gearbox, a faulty setting. And as he spoke I massaged the finger. And when he stopped talking I opened my hands and released him. The finger was whole …

Badrallach, Kilmore,

Llanfaethlu, Llanfechell,

Kincardine, Kinross,

Loughcarron, Loughgelly …

We caroused right through the night. Toasts to the landlord who claimed he met my father once and as the night went on that they were close friends. Toasts to Teddy and Gracie. Toasts to my return. To Donal's finger. Toasts to the departed groom and his prowess. To the bride and her fertility. To the rich harvest – the corn, the wheat, the barley. Toasts to all Septembers and all harvests and to all things ripe and eager for the reaper. A Dionysian night. A Bacchanalian night. A frenzied, excessive Irish night when ritual was consciously and relentlessly debauched.

Then sometime before dawn McGarvey was remembered. Their greatest, their closest friend McGarvey who in his time had danced with them and drunk with them and built roads with them and cut turf with them. McGarvey who ought to have been best man that day – my God, who else? – and who wasn't even at the wedding reception. And as they created him I saw McGarvey in my mind, saw his strained face and his mauve hands and his burning eyes, crouched in his wheelchair and sick with bitterness. Saw him and knew him before Teddy in his English innocence asked why he wasn't there; before Ned told us of the fall from the scaffolding and the paralysis. Saw him and recognized our meeting: an open place, a walled yard, trees, orange skies, warm wind. And knew, knew with cold certainty that nothing was going to happen. Nothing at all.

McKeever is a middle-aged undertaker trying to stage a production of *A Midsummer Night's Dream* in Ballintra – a seaside village in the South of Ireland. McKeever has had an affair with Elizabeth Langton – the daughter of Reverend and Mrs Langton – who is considerably younger than himself. The relationship has ended five years previously. Elizabeth has returned to Ballintra to see her dying mother. On Easter Sunday, Mrs Langton is dead and McKeever is preparing her body in his embalming studio.

Moonshine *by Jim Nolan*

McKeever

Enfin, le visage! Hands and face, the most important. Visible signs, d'y'see. So. No cock-ups in that department. And there won't be either – not tonight, Josephine! (*Water and cloth at base of trolley*) The embalmer, Margaret, is a creator of illusions. We banish the traces of suffering and death and present the deceased in an attitude of normal and restful sleep. We create, as Strub and Frederick so movingly put it, 'a memory picture'. Good old Strub and Frederick, the unsung heroes of the mortuary. Perhaps you've heard of them, Margaret. Their book, *The Principles and*

Practice of Embalming is the veritable bible of our profession. Not exactly coffee table stuff, I grant you, and I don't expect they'll surface in the bestseller lists, but old Strub and Frederick have filled many a lonely hour for me, I can tell you. (*Pause*) There now, clean as a new pin. (*Forceps and cotton wool*) Next, we have the packing of the orifices. Don't worry, Margaret, you won't feel a thing. (*Pause*) You don't mind if I call you Margaret, do you, Margaret? I feel it brings us closer. And after all, I was almost one of the family one time, wasn't I? Of course, you couldn't have known that and I don't suppose it matters to you now but I was, yes, very much so.

Pause. Takes remote control switch from pocket and turns off music.

We were lovers, y'see. Lizzie and me. That shocked you, didn't it – if you were alive today you'd die of the fright. Yes, lovers. In this very room too. On this very trolley. Life and death. Would have told you sooner only I didn't think you'd understand. That's why she went away. Nothing to do with you or John, Margaret – it was all McKeever's fault. (*Pause*) Don't be angry, Margaret – I meant no harm. Please. Don't get upset. It was all right. (*Pause*) It was all right, that is, until I blew it. I couldn't cut it, Margaret. And the track record, not great. Ask the absent Mrs McKeever if you don't believe me. Didn't want to repeat history, did we? So I rewrote it instead. Our father who art in exile, that was me. Never around when he's wanted.

(*Sings*) I see the moon, the moon sees me
Under the shade of the old oak tree.
Please let the moon that shines on me
Shine on the one I love.

The Lord is a down-and-out Dublin man who makes what money he can by helping motorists find parking spaces. He lives in a men's hostel and drinks wine from a bottle in his pocket. In the past, he had a wife, children, a shop, a home and was a part-time drummer in a band. Twelve years ago, however, The Lord was playing for the wedding of a County Councillor, when a tragic turn of events changed his life forever. He befriends Seán, a man from the hostel who has just been thrown out of a squat. Here, he tells him about the day he lost everything.

A Picture of Paradise *by Jimmy Murphy*

The Lord

An hour … that's how much I missed them by … one poxy hour. (...)

If I'd've left on time I'd've been back in time … to … We were playing that gig in Wicklow, a wedding. I'd promised her I'd drive straight home after it. (*Pause.*) This eegit, the big thick muckah that got married, came backstage for a photo with the band, then wanted to buy us a drink. (*Pause.*) Just one drink, that was all I said I'd have … just the one. Two hours went by before I looked at me watch. (*Pause.*) I was pissed drunk. The weather was bitter that night … black ice everywhere on the road. (*Pause.*) She used to light the gas fire before going to bed to heat the house for me after the long drive back from the gigs. (*Long pause.*) I remember the fire engines passing me at Islandbridge, three of them. I was stopped at the lights at Knockmaroon hill and could see flames leaping up into the sky, clouds of black smoke and sparks bursting up into the air. (*Pause.*) The flashing lights of the ambulance and fire engines had me dizzy as I drove up to the house. A Guard stopped me and told me there was no traffic being let through. (*Pause.*) He smelt the drink off me … kept me in the car while a breathalyser was got. When I got out of the car to give him me name and address I saw a roof blazing … our roof. All the neighbours were out with blankets over their shoulders. 'You drunken bastard', I heard someone shout. (*Pause.*) One of the kids … must've been Nora, left a teddy bear near the fire. 'Teddy Johnson', that's what she called him. (*Pause.*) That's what they said was the cause of it. (*Takes out the photos and looks at them.*) Nothing left of them but ashes. (...)

I've played that gig in me head a million times … each time that thick asks us in for a drink I smash his head in … I make it home just in time.

The Bishop has taken the unusual measure of making a visit to Carraigthomond – a small town in the South-West of Ireland – to deliver this sermon. A man visiting from England has been found beaten to death in a field. This field had been the subject of an argument between the dead man and a local farmer – Bull McCabe. Everyone in the parish knows that the Bull is responsible for the murder but no-one is willing to speak up for fear of repercussions. At Mass one Sunday, the Bishop makes this plea.

The Field *by John B. Keane*

The Bishop

Five weeks ago in this parish, a man was murdered – he was brutally beaten to death. For five weeks the police have investigated and not one single person has come forward to assist them. Everywhere they turned, they were met by silence, a silence of the most frightful and diabolical kind – the silence of the lie. In God's name, I beg you, I implore you, if any of you knows anything, to come forward and to speak without fear.

This is a parish in which you understand hunger. But there are many hungers. There is a hunger for food – a natural hunger. There is the hunger of the flesh – a natural understandable hunger. There is a hunger for home, for love, for children. These things are good – they are good because they are necessary. But there is also the hunger for land. And in this parish, you, and your fathers before you knew what it was to starve because you did not own your own land – and that has increased; this unappeasable hunger for land. But how far are you prepared to go to satisfy this hunger. Are you prepared to go to the point of robbery? Are you prepared to go to the point of murder? Are you prepared to kill for land? Was this man killed for land? Did he give his life's blood for a field? If so, that field will be a field of blood and it will be paid for in thirty pieces of silver – the price of Christ's betrayal – and you, by your silence will share in that betrayal.

Among you there is a murderer! You may even know his name, you may even have seen him commit this terrible crime – through your silence, you share his guilt, your innocent children will grow up under the shadow of this terrible crime, and you will carry this guilt with you until you face your Maker at the moment of judgement …

If you are afraid to go to the police, then come to your priests, or come to me. And if there is one man among you – one man made after Christ's likeness – he will stand up and say: 'There! There he is! There is the murderer!' And that man will have acknowledged Christ before men and Christ will acknowledge him before His Father in Heaven. But if you, by your silence, deny Christ before men, He will disown you in Heaven, and I, as His representative, will have a solemn duty to perform. I will place this parish under interdict and then there will be a silence more terrible than the first. The church bell will be silent: the mass bell will not be heard; the voice of the confessional will be stilled and in your last moment will be the most dreadful silence of all for you will go to face your Maker without the last sacrament on your lips … and all because of your silence now. In God's name, I beg of you to speak before it is too late. 'I am the way, says Christ, and the truth. Do not be afraid of those who can kill the body but cannot kill the soul. But rather, be afraid of him who can destroy both body and soul in hell'.

In the name of the Father and of the Son and of the Holy Ghost, Amen.

Andy Tracey, aged fifty, is a joiner by trade. He has recently married Hanna Wilson, a woman in her late-forties, and finds himself living with her mother, instead of in their new house at Riverview. This arrangement was supposed to have been a temporary one, but his mother-in-law is keen to keep the newly-weds with her. Mrs Wilson has a devout fondness for St Philomena. She insists on Andy and Hanna joining herself and her equally pious neighbour, Cissy Cassidy, each evening for the Rosary. In this speech, he is sitting in the back yard, speaking directly and confidentially to the audience about the day he discovered the truth about St Philomena!

Lovers: Losers *by Brian Friel*

Andy

And then there was the Rosary caper. Well, I mean to say, a man has to draw the line somewhere. Oh, no, says I; we may have to stay together of necessity, says I, but by God it won't be because we pray together; I'll say my own mouthful of prayers down here. And that settled that. I mean to say a man has to take a stand some time. No harm to Father U.S.A. Peyton, says I; but all things in their proper place, and the proper place for me and my missus is in Riverview. I'll manage rightly down here, says I; and Father Peyton and Saint Philomena and the three sorrowful mysteries can hammer away upstairs. She didn't like that, the aul' woman, I'll tell you. Didn't speak to me for weeks. And would you believe what she done on me to get her own back: it was Cissy told me with a wee toss of her head. 'She offered you up to Saint Philomena,' says she. Crafty? Oh, man! Hanna's thick – there's no denying that; but she'll never have the craft of the aul' woman.

But I got her! By God I got her! … or I damn near got her. It was this day in the works – a Friday – I'll never forget it – and George Williamson comes sidling up to me with a newspaper in his hand and a great aul' smirk on his jaw, and says he, 'So the Pope's not infallible after all, Andy,' says he. Oh, a bad bitter Protestant, the same Williamson. 'What's that?' says I, you know there, very quiet. 'According to the paper here,' says he, 'even the Pope can make a mistake. What d'you make of that now, eh? Isn't that a surprise?' And he hands me the paper. So I pulls out the glasses, very calm, and puts them on, and takes the paper from him and looks at it. And true as Christ, when I seen it, you could have tipped me over, I was that weak. Like, for five seconds, I couldn't even speak with excitement; only the heart thumping like bloody hell in my chest. For there it was in black and white before my very eyes: THE SAINT THAT NEVER WAS. 'Official Vatican sources today announced' – I know it by heart – 'that the devotion of all Roman Catholics to Saint Philomena must be discontinued at once because there is little or no evidence that such a person ever existed.' Like I never knew I was a spiteful man until that minute; and then, by God, my only thought was to stick that paper down the aul' woman's throat. Poor Williamson – Christ, I shot past him like a scalded cat and out of the workshop like the hammers of hell.

What I should have done – like, I know now – my God, no need to tell me; instead of coopering things up the way I done – but what I should have done was wait until after the tea and then go upstairs nice and calm, you know there, and sit down on the side of the bed very pleasant, and say, 'Have a look through the paper there, Mrs. Wilson,' and watch, by God, watch every wee flicker of her eye when she'd come to the big news … but I bollixed it. I know. I know. I bollixed it. Straight from the workshop into a pub. And when closing time comes, there I am – blotto. And back to the house singing and shouting like a madman.

Irish Man is a fifty-one year old, self-made property developer who does not divulge his name. He is disillusioned with his life and obsessed by his desperate desire to sing like the opera singer, Gigli. This is his fourth meeting with JPW King, a healer whom he visits looking for help. The Irish Man's wife and son have just left him, fearing that his emotional outbursts will end in violence. He is hungover and, here, responds to King's question about his first time to have sex – an encounter that took place when he was twenty-two.

The Gigli Concert *by Tom Murphy*

Irish Man

I got very excited, and I almost ran, hurrying home to tell Danny. Danny was next in age to me, I was the youngest and I think he was always a bit embarrassed by my – innocence, I think. He was asleep, but I was proud of myself and I wanted to tell him so that he'd see I wasn't a fool. And I woke him up and told him I'd – had it. And he just rolled over and said, 'how many times' and went back to sleep ... You see, Danny (*'There's a story.'*) ... You see, my eldest brother had singled out Danny as the one to be put through school, educated. But I don't think school suited our Danny. But I don't think my eldest brother wanted to admit that. But my father sick, and then dying, and my eldest brother had took over, and he become a sort of tyrant. (...)

Mick. Mick frightened us all. Shouting, kicking his bike. Kicking the doors, shouting. My mother thought the world of him. He used to parade his learning too. 'Can anyone tell me what was St Bernadette's second name?' 'Soubrou', or whatever it was. Imagine, he used to give Danny tests. In arithmetic, I suppose. And I'd be sitting quietly, hoping that Danny, locked upstairs in that room, would pass Mick's examination paper … And Danny was always trying to teach me – cunning, I think. Street sense. He used to tell me never trust anyone, and that everything is based on hate. He used to tell me that when I got big, if I was ever in a fight with Mick, to watch out, that Mick would use a poker. I suppose he knew he'd never be able for Mick, unless he shot him, or knifed him. But we didn't do things that way … I wanted to be a priest. I was crazy, I was thirteen. But some notion in my head about – dedicating? – my life to others. But Mick, in consultation with my mother – and rightly so – said wait a couple of years. And one day – and the couple of years weren't up – and Mick was in a black mood. And he'd beaten Danny that day too for something or other, and I had went outside. Oh, just outside, sitting on the patch of grass. And. There's only two flowers for children from my kind of background. The daisy and the … the yellow one. (...)

The primrose too – the buttercup. Oh, just sitting there, picking them off the grass. And Mick come out. What about the priesthood, he said. I'd changed my mind but I didn't tell him. I said – I stood up. The couple of years isn't up I said. But he knew I'd changed my mind and he said you're stupid, and he flattened me. I knew what he was at, I was learning. That day the priesthood would've gave the family a bit of status. But unfortunately for the family, that day I'd changed my mind … Oh yes, the flowers. And. I still had this little bunch of flowers. In my hand. I don't think I gave a fuck about the flowers. A few – daisies, and the – yellow ones. But Danny – he was eighteen! – and he was inside, crying. And it was the only thing I could think of. (*He is only just managing to hold back his tears.*) And. And. I took the fuckin' flowers to our Danny … wherever he is now … and I said, which do you think is nicest? The most beautiful, yeh know? And Danny said 'Nicest?', like a knife. 'Nicest? Are you stupid? What use is nicest?' Of what use is beauty, Mr King?

Chris Farrell is an ex-airline pilot. He has a drink problem and – having never married – seems somewhat lonely. At the airport, he runs into the Fox family – old neighbours from suburban Dublin whom he has not seen for twenty years. Frank and Julie Fox are welcoming home their daughter, Joelle, who is now living in America. Julie reminds Chris about a rake he borrowed many years previously and never returned. Despite their rudeness, Chris is unfailingly apologetic and polite, even giving Julie a blank cheque for the rake! He follows them to their home with a bottle of champagne and a drinking session ensues. It is now three a.m. Joelle has gone to bed, while Frank and Julie have decided they are tired of Chris. After humiliating him, they abruptly tell him to leave their house. Chris tells the Foxes what he really thinks of them, during which Joelle comes downstairs.

Down Onto Blue *by Pom Boyd*

Chris

I just wanted … I just thought … I was lonely … I just wanted some warmth, a bit of life. I thought to be with a family at a happy time, to share … but … My god! You're sick! You are sick people. You don't love anybody! You don't even love each other. (*Shouting*) Joelle! Joelle! get out of this house, it's full of sick people! Get out now while you can! (...)

And as for your rake. You think I don't remember? You think I don't recall? Well I do. Of course I do. But I didn't wish to say. Would never have said. But now I will. Now I'll tell you what I remember about your precious rake Julie. I remember it very clearly, it had as you said light springy prongs on it and if I'm not mistaken a green handle. Anyway I did as a matter of fact try to leave it back, to put it in the garden shed as I had promised. It was late October, November, I'd needed it for the leaves, my own had disappeared. Anyway I found I was prevented from leaving it back. Do you know why Julie? Joelle do you? (*Joey shakes her head tersely*) Well when I got there I heard noises, small little movements coming from inside. (*Puts his hand to his ear*) Wha's tha? I didn't know. Maybe a rat, maybe a dog but I didn't expect to see what I saw....What did I see? I saw *(Making a grand gesture)* I saw this little girl, your daughter, in her white vest and pants sitting there with her book on the stone floor beside the lawn mower. She was cold and in the dim light I could make out red marks on her legs but she was not crying. She told me that you, Julie had put her there and that she was to stay there till bed time. I asked her if she thought I should bolt the door again and she said she thought I should. So I did ... and I did not leave the rake. I must say, I was in a dilemma. I couldn't leave it outside in case it was nicked but if I left it in the shed you would have known that I had ... seen. I knew Frank you would have been ... put out, embarrassed perhaps, if you had known I had walked in on such a personal matter. Now I think I'll go. I never thought I would intrude on a family in this way ... I believe the family is sacred. Yes I do. Joelle, you're a wonderful girl. You'll bring quality and class wherever you go. Good night to you. (*He exits*)

Scober (Barney) McAdam is fifty-nine years old. He comes originally from a very poor background but now owns Clonhaggard, a large mountainy farm in Leitrim. By the late 1950s, he is successful and married to Tressa, a woman less than half his age. He is forced to tolerate constant jibes from other men in the village insinuating that he is sexually impotent. Maguire, a neighbouring small farmer, upsets Tressa by questioning her about her marriage and her lack of children. Tressa tells Scober that he is not respected by Maguire. This is his response.

King of the Castle *by Eugene McCabe*

Scober

He's jealous – That's respect. Jealous, 'cause I've worked – used my head – put lorries on the road – got this place and others, bought out most of the mountain – planted timber, built barns, roofed yards – I employ men – I have a young wife. (*Pause, pointing up*) Electric. (*Longish pause*) I was in rags at school with all of them – but you've got to stay that way – raggy, stupid and poor – 'Ah! sure it's a hard life' and 'How can a man live where snipes starve?' 'But won't we get our reward afterwards?' – Slobber! (*Pointing out*) There's a ton of barley to the acre from three inches of soil out there – stones, a lot of it – and there's men in Meath on the fattest land in Ireland'd lie happy with a yield like that, and still the fools'd starve before they'd ask, 'How's it done?' 'Can I do-it?' – Spite! Ignorance! Envy! Let 'em starve – let 'em live on spite and take the boat – rotten thatch with lumps of grass – all sunk away from the chimneys – windows that leave it dusk inside of a summer's day – the dung-heap and the bony cow – the messy yard and the few mousey sheep – I was born to it – know every hour of it – the waste, the crownshawning by the fire in winter – Everything to blame but themselves and 'cause they don't do anything – like Maguire, they've time to watch – Every turf you save and lamb you mark – the lorries that come and go – they count and question and what they don't know they guess, and if man improves – they say, 'No man bests the mountain 'less he's a thief like Bull Haggard.' But if you work and deal and best the mountain – you've made *dirt* of them – and that's what they hate – order – yields – business, the power to buy – (...)

Hundreds of years – we've scraped those rocks – the graveyards full of MacAdams – Tobins – Mullarkeys – lived and died – lek scarecrows. When I was a cub I could see this place – these windows lit up like a ship. Now I look out of them.

Matt Talbot – a Dublin historical figure – is an unskilled worker and devout Catholic. Born in 1856 – the second of twelve children – he grew up in savage poverty and became an alcoholic. When he was twenty-eight, he underwent a remarkable change, imposing on himself a vigorous regime of fasting, prayer and total abstinence from alcohol. He also secretly bound his body with chains and cords as a penance. A movement for his canonisation began soon after his death in 1925. Here – towards the end of his life – he is talking to his sister, Susan, who is desperately worried about the state of his health and upset by his lack of regard for her concerns.

Talbot's Box *by Thomas Kilroy*

Talbot

The way to God was be giving up them that's nearest to me. 'Twas what Our Lord said to the fishermen, y'see. But then I discovered something strange, Susan. (*She begins to move away.*) Having given all up, it was all given back to me, but different, y'know what I mean. All the world and the people in the world came back to me in me own room. But everything in place. Nothing twisted 'n broken as it is in this world. Everything straight as a piece of good timber, without warp. (*Looks about. Alone.*) Susie! Susie! There's something in me that makes it hard for others to abide me. Even me own. (*Prayer.*) Oh, Lord. Help me to prepare myself that I may know my sins. Let thy light shine upon my darkness! I was cranky with Susan today. Or was it yesterday? No matter. Sometime recent it was. The auld spite risin' up in me again against me own father. When what I was hatin' was the drunkard that was in meself. Who am I to say what good or bad is in another? There was that strange thing in the book I was reading. What was it? About the holy men 'n women who went out into the deserts of Egypt. It says in the book they were waiting for the end of the world. The coming of the New Jerusalem! 'N they thought to end the world quicker be taking the vow of virginity. No more little childer! I dunno. I think there's always 'n will be always some sorta urge in human-kind to end its breeding. (*Memory.*) There was that girl, wance, who talked to me about them things. Lizzie! It was such a long time ago. She used to be in service. In a Protestant rectory she was. 'N the priest said I did right. I walked away from her. Ya chose a higher love, Matt, the priest said. (*Upset.*) Higher or lower, can ya measure it with a ruler? She said I was going agin me own nature. Isn't it a quare thing the way the body does stand in the way of Eternity? The time will come, says the Lord, when the body, that garment of shame shall be cast off 'n there will be no more male 'n female. (*Pause. Irritation.*) That being so, wasn't it a strange thing to make us men 'n women in the first place! Kneel down with ya! (*Kneels.*) Bless me father, for I have sinned!

Thomas Dunne is in his seventies and lives in the county home in Baltinglass in 1932. He once held the rank of Chief Superintendent with the Dublin Metropolitan Police – the highest level a Catholic could reach in that force. His wife had borne him four children – one boy and three girls – before she died in childbirth. His son, Willie, was killed in France during World War I. When Thomas' mind began to wander, he became too much for his daughter, Annie, to handle and was sent to the county home. In his mind, the past mingles freely with the present. Here – as often happens in his bare room – his son appears as a thirteen-year-old boy and sings to him.

The Steward of Christendom

by Sebastian Barry

Thomas

My poor son … When I was a small child, smaller than yourself, my Ma Ma brought me home a red fire engine from Baltinglass. It was wrapped in the newspaper and hid in the hayshed for the Christmas. But I knew every nook and cranny of the hayshed, and I soon had it found, and the paper off it. And quite shortly I had invented a grand game, where I stood one foot on the engine and propelled myself across the yard. I kept falling and falling, tearing and scumming my clothes, but no matter, the game was a splendid game. And my mother she came out for something, maybe to fling the grains at the hens in that evening time, and she saw me skating on the engine and she looked at me. She looked with a terrible long face, and I looked down and there was the lovely engine all scratched and bent, and the wheel half-rubbed off it. So she took the toy quietly from under my foot, and marched over to the dunghill and shoved it in deep with her bare hands, tearing at the rubbish there and the layers of dung. So I sought out her favourite laying hen and put a yard-bucket over it, and it wasn't found for a week, by which time the Christmas was over and the poor hen's wits had gone astray from hunger and darkness and inertia. Nor did it ever lay eggs again that quickened with chicks. And that was a black time between my Ma Ma and me. (*After a little.*) You were six when your Mam died, Willie. Hardly enough time to be at war with her, the way a son might. She was very attached to you. Her son. She had a special way of talking about you, a special music in her voice. And she was proud of your singing, and knew you could make a go of it, in the halls, if you wished. I wanted to kill her when she said that. But at six you sang like a linnet, true enough. (*After a little.*) I didn't do as well as she did, with you. I was sorry you never reached six feet. I was a fool. What big loud talking fools are fathers sometimes. Why do we not love our sons simply and be done with it? She did. I would kill, or I would do a great thing, just to see you once more, in the flesh. All I got back was your uniform, with the mud only half-washed out of it. Why do they send the uniforms to the fathers and the mothers? I put it over my head and cried for a night, like an owl in a tree. I cried for a night with your uniform over my head, and no one saw me.